CU01011327

DARLING IVY

A Love Story in Letters

Muriel Bridgewater

Book Guild Publishing
Sussex, England

First published in Great Britain in 2010 by
The Book Guild Ltd
Pavilion View
19 New Road
Brighton, BN1 1UF

Typesetting by Ellipsis Books Ltd, Glasgow

Printed in Great Britain by
CPI Anthony Rowe

A catalogue record for this book is available from
The British Library.

ISBN 978 1 84624 482 7

To our parents, Ivy and Ken,
who made us who we are.

Contents

Preface

Ivy Ross and Ken Bridgewater started courting in 1931 and married in December 1938. At the time of their marriage Ken was 26 and Ivy 25. According to their marriage certificate, Ken was a 'bread salesman' and Ivy a 'pickle factory clerk'.

Ivy and Ken had four children, Linda, Muriel, Lorna and Jennifer, three of whom were born during the Second World War.

Ivy and Ken were married for almost 39 years before Ken was struck down with a fatal heart attack at the age of 64 – ironically just two months before he was due to retire. Ivy lived alone for a further 29 years; the much-loved kingpin of her family. She was an incredibly strong, wise and independent lady who dealt stoically with all that life could throw at her.

Ivy and Ken's love affair with one another endured through many years of separation and hardship. Ken was on active service in Italy during the War and, following that, the urgent need to earn money forced him to seek work away from home.

Ken was employed initially, and briefly, by a number of small engineering firms operating in the North of England before joining British Timken. His work with them carried him abroad once again and he spent many years working, and living, in Italy, Germany and Switzerland.

After being made redundant in 1958 Ken, at last, found work at home. Much to Ivy's delight, he took the necessary examinations to enable him to set up his own driving school and ran a very successful business from home for several years.

The letters that tell their story were not discovered until after Ivy's death in 2005. No trace of Ivy's letters to Ken has ever come to light, although it is clear that many were written and that Ken looked forward longingly to their arrival.

The letters, unseen before by their daughters, shed so much light on Ivy and Ken's private relationship. Muriel, in an earlier book about her childhood (*Flying Off The Shed Roof*), had imagined her parents might be either poor or 'straight-laced'.

'Were Mom and Dad poor or did they think themselves too genteel for such diversions? All I can remember in our own flat was a very crackly radio for adult use only.'

It was humbling to realise that their inhibitions had been caused by their very straitened circumstances.

There is a constant thread running through the letters voicing concern about the lack of money, the lack of work and 'managing'. In adulthood, Linda, Muriel, Lorna and Jennifer found these revelations heartbreaking. At the same time, however, Ivy and Ken's triumph over their struggles engendered a feeling of fierce pride in the girls for their parents.

Darling Ivy is, essentially, a love story: a love story that transcended everything and one that gave Ivy and Ken's children the framework that they needed to live their own lives in a meaningful way – to be as successful, hard-working, reliable, honest and compassionate as their parents had always striven to be.

A Note on Punctuation

In an endeavour to keep Ken's letters as original as possible, his exact grammar, punctuation, capitalisation and so on have been authentically reproduced.

Improper nouns and adjectives sometimes have capital letters, as in: 'Percy is not as fast as us on Bumpy corners . . .'

Words are often enclosed by double quotation marks for no apparent reason and the apostrophe is used with great abandon to indicate the omission of one or more letters at the beginning of many words. Ken would often write (and say) such things as '*'orrible with a capital apostrophe*'; and no one used more artificial exclamation marks

– or more emphatic underlining – than he did to demonstrate a point.

Today's texters would probably favour a few of Ken's shortened words: 'nowt' for nothing, 'em' for them, 'wot' for what, and so on.

His copperplate handwriting was superb and he was a terrific raconteur who regularly had articles printed in magazines and newspapers. He often signed his letters to his children with a quick sketch of a chubby lion's paw, complete with sharp claws. This was his shorthand for 'Paw', Pa, Daddy or Dad.

Ken was, in fact, a stickler for correct grammar and spelling. He began school in 1917 when the English language was still of paramount importance, whether written or spoken. Today's readers may find his use of grammar and punctuation a little strange but almost 100 years have passed since he was born and many of the 'rules', and indeed the meanings of words, have changed during the century.

1

Courting

172 Aldridge Road
Perry Barr, Birmingham

Beloved,

I only received your letter today. It was wonderful darling! Will you write again! I wish you would! It's so lonely without you dear. You have at least some diversions to while away the time, whilst I am back to grim realization!

I arrived home at 10.20 and I've been waiting for a letter ever since.

Yes darling I possess a pen, but I'm in the car, and anyway, I left the pen at home so you'll have to forgive me.

I'm sorry I couldn't stay to tea dear, but of course you understand don't you. I should have loved to, but a promise is a promise.

Had a good journey home, but didn't see Len, although I met George Lester on the top of the Horse Shoe Pass.

By the way darling, the A.C.S. ite I told you about was George Anscombe.

Went to Barmouth on Sunday, and it rained like 'Ell for 90 miles. There's one road over the mountain (Cader Idris) which rises 1,450 feet in 2,553 yards. Gradient of 1-7 and 1-4. Like this.

The engine boiled and took 40 mins to cool.

Yes darling I still love you. But I wish you were back. I have had to come all the way back from Barmouth alone, and to while away the time, I waved to all the girls. There! I always tell you everything, because I love you! After all, taint very thrilling waving to girls at 40 m.p.h.

Had your photograph stuck on the windscreen, just to remind me that if I drove dangerously, I might break somebody's heart.

Well dear, I can't think of much to write, although I couldn't tell you enough times how much I love you.

(The author paused here to wither a charming young lady on the opposite corner with a baleful glance.) She's tried to "get off", fast cat.

Took Mapankathanesmee a ride yesterday, went to Ludlow and Tenbury, couldn't come to Rhyl again. When I come next week dear, I shall come through Wrexham. (No I'm sorry I shan't.) I forgot for a moment that I'd got to go to Blackpool! (Pause here to ignite the fragrant weed.)

Please darling, don't worry about me! Have a good time, flirt if you like, but don't forget to leg-pull when it gets too hot. I love you. Keep off the chocolates dearest! Don't spoil your wonderful looks before you get back. And <u>don't</u> bring me any rock back, because I hate it! No darling, I'm not being presumptuous, but – I know you! And I wouldn't offend you for all the world.

Ask your Dad what he thinks about the infallibility of the Pope? And if he's ever been to Llandfairpwyllgwyngthgwagueerythgwing-wroglethlandosillyogogogwyth Charming place, tortorbeadnit?

After reviewing the above, I find that it's all twattle (!!!!) so I'll just try and tell you again how much I love you. You do believe me sweetheart. You must, and remember that I trust you, just as . . .

(Frustratingly, there is a page missing here.)

. . . 10.45. Even if it's only just one kiss dear, it will revive me.

<u>Sunday</u> same arrangement from 8 o'clock to 10 o'clock. But I promise nothing!

Barring the above, will you come down on Monday at 7 o'clock?

Must ring off now dear, but please, please write again. Your letter was divine dear, I shall keep it for ever.

Best of love, always dearest, from your loving sweetheart.

Kenneth x x x

PS: Give enclosure to your mother.
      All my Love for ever "say a little prayer for me".

Ken and his sister Kath used many made-up words and phrases in their correspondence as well as in their everyday language. Some are still used by the family. For example, Bank Holiday Monday has always been Monk Holiday Bandy.

Ken writes 'Mapankathanesmee' rather than the cumbersome 'Ma and Pa and Kath and Esmee'. He also uses 'tortorbeadnit' – 'it ought to be hadn't it?'

He apologises for using a pencil. It was considered bad form. Ken did have the most amazingly beautiful handwriting and invariably used a Parker fountain pen, which he refilled from a bottle of Quink ink, kept in the bureau. He was also able to do very quick sketches to demonstrate a point.

The expression 'must ring off' is a strange one as he was writing, not telephoning.

'The fragrant weed' refers to cigarettes. Ken had a lifelong affair with smoking. He did hate seaside rock though; if a stick came his way he would store it in the sideboard until it had become soft before grudgingly biting off a piece.

172 Aldridge Road

Jan 20th 31

Dear Ivy

I am sorry I have not been able to see you lately but I have been so busy I have not even had time to write until tonight.

I have started work again, and am getting on very well. It is at R C Bradley & Sons, Wholesale Tobacconists, Digbeth.

I work with two other boys, both decent sports.

On Tuesday afternoon the conversation naturally turned to girls. I said I knew a great little girl (meaning you), and this other boy said that he did. After arguing for about 10 minutes, each saying that the other was no judge of girls etc. I asked him where he lived, and he said Lozells. (Previous to this mind you, I had been trying to remember where I had heard his surname before.) The next question I asked was where the girl lived and the answer was, Crompton Road! I immediately "opened my eyes", and decided to be diplomatic. I said "Are you going out with this girl regularly?" and he said "No! some kid named Ken is going out with her and I haven't got a chance while he's around."

And now at this juncture I remembered his name, "Good Lord", I said "Is your name Leonard?" and it was, -------- Leonard Ruthers!

At this stage I thought the joke had gone far enough, so I asked him if he lived at No.17 and he said "You".

Then suddenly, he realised it, and said "Good God are you Ken?" (His very words), "How small the world is."

I had previously shown him that snap of you, and he said he <u>thought</u> he recognised you. Well it's rather difficult to explain a thing like this hurriedly but I've done my best, and I'll bet you're somewhat surprised.

To think that we both talked about a <u>"smashing girl"</u> and according to me, mine was better than his, and according to him, his was the best, and all the time it was the same one, namely: Ivy Ross.

6

You'll no doubt be pleased to know that we're not bitter enemies over this matter, but alternatively, the best of friends.

Len has got one or two rather funny peculiarities, but other wise he is a very good sport.

It seems ages since I saw you, and the trouble is I cannot really say when I can see you again, as it will have to be after 8 o'clock. I'll tell you what, could you see me on Wednesday at 8 o'clock at your house?

Hoping that you are well. I will close as I am in a hurry now.

Yours with Love

Kenneth x x x

PS You know that I never write in pencil unless I'm in a desperate hurry and I'm sure you'll excuse it won't you? That is if you can read it.

Ken x

Ivy in the garden of her parents' house, 1931

Where do you hide

Yourself these days?

K

This note, dated in Roman numerals (1 May 1931), was written in large characters on a single sheet of paper.

Ivy kept it amongst her letters; it shows signs of much folding and unfolding, being nearly worn through at the creases.

"Roselea"

Ivy Darling

Try and make it 6.15p.m. tonight there's a dear, and I'll be up on the mark.
How are you? "Oak"?

Best Love

always from

Kenneth x x

'Roselea' is 172 Aldridge Road, Perry Barr, Birmingham. This was Ken's parents' house and his home until his marriage in 1938. When his mother, Rosy, died in March 1949 Ken, Ivy and their four young daughters moved into Roselea and made it their family home for several years.

'Oak' is another family expression used instead of OK.

Lindens

Darling,

Herewith your ticket for Donnington.
Don't lose it.
Just come in an ordinary morning frock. Many people will be in leathers and flannels. Make it a nice frock and try to look posh.
Never mind about the people you meet. There are no snobs.
I don't know where I shall be at Donnington but get Wal to find the "Marshals" parking place, and wait till I find you.
Thanks for express letter – twas marvellous.
Am in great hurry now dear to catch post.
So tons of Love Darling until tomorrow when we can hold one another again.

Love always

Your Own

Ken

Tell Mom you won't be home until 2am about on Sunday. We shall not stop the night. This will save 18/-

All my Love

Darling

Xxx

'Lindens' was a hotel in Llandrindod Wells. Unusually, this note was undated; the content indicates the most likely date to be early 1930s.

Ken had a lifelong interest in motorbikes and owned many of the famous old British bikes such as Norton and Triumph at one time or another. It seems he marshalled for races held at Donnington Park from time to time. Ivy rode pillion and travelled to Wales, Scotland and Cornwall on the back of the bike. She cut a fine dash in her flying goggles, leather helmet and long coat.

Will you do me a favour darling and send me a telegram as soon as you get home on Sunday night? You can send it from the 'phone box for 6d. I have mapped one out that will go for 6d:-

BRIDGEWATER. LINDENS PRIVATE HOTEL.
SPA ROAD. LLANDRINDOD-WELLS.
SAFE ARRIVAL. LOVE IVY.

If you do this darling say at even 11pm. I shall certainly get it for Monday morning so please put my heart at rest.

If you get a chance remind Wal that Percy is not so fast as us on Bumpy corners, and ask him not to overdo it because you know your kid takes risks.

Don't forget sweetheart that any letter you send me <u>after Friday</u> will have to be sent to Llandrindod Wells. So if you write on Saturday send it to the Hotel.

Wal was a biker friend who was chosen to be best man at Ivy and Ken's wedding. Wal and his wife, Vera, remained firm friends with Ivy and Ken for many, many years.

Percy, nicknamed 'your kid' in this letter, was Ivy's brother. He was, in fact, older than Ivy by some years. He and Ken were also firm friends for life and supported one another in any number of ways – whether it was financially, practically or emotionally.

Percy kept a watchful eye over the 'nibs' (Linda, Muriel, Lorna and Jennifer) following Ken's premature death in May 1977.

523 Tyburn Road   July 5th 1937
Erdington, Birmingham

Darling,

I did not send you a card my dear, as I knew you would get a letter as soon, and I did not want to tell everyone at the digs how much I love you.

Wal and I arrived at home OK at about 10.15. We had about 75 minutes stops. Wal's wire to the battery broke, and we had to mend it. Don't tell Wal this: – and don't worry about it, but his motor seized three times. I am going to have a look at it tonight. I am not going to the pictures.

I am missing you terribly already darling, and have a kind of hollow feeling in my tummy. I left two spuds at dinner time, and Mrs E says I've gone off my grub. So I've just made up for it and ate up all the Sunday scraps for my tea. Break here to see a client.

The said client has just told me that he wants to buy a £750 house thro the Prudential. Cheers!

I have put the camera in post dear, and there is a film in it, wind it carefully to No.1. When you have used it, ask the man at the shop to fit a new one and tell him you wouldn't sell the camera for £10.

I hope your Eye is better darling, please let me know.

Have a good time sweetheart and don't forget that I love you. I slept in your bed last night dear.

I am sorry dear, but I have got to rush out so I must close, but I will send you a long letter soon.

Be a good girl darling, and look after Doll. Please don't stay up too late.

Tons of love dear one from your own Ken with Love Xxxxxxxxx
Please write soon dear as I miss you so

Your Ken

523 Tyburn Road was Ken's place of work at the time. It seems from the letter that he was working for the Prudential Assurance Company for a while.

Doll was Ivy's youngest sister. Although Ivy had three other sisters it was mostly Doll that she spent her leisure time with. They were the closest to one another in age. Throughout their lives they continued to go on holiday together to far-away places such as Canada, America and Spain.

Ivy and Doll in Llandudno, 1937

Dear Ivy

Arrived home quite safely after rather a miserable journey all on my lonesome. I had almost the train to myself all the way down. I suppose if I had had my better half with me, it would have been crammed.

Well duckie, how are you? All OK again and happy. I was sorry when I heard you had fallen out, and I felt so sorry for your poor boy, he was heartbroken. My dear, can't you make up your mind whether you want him or not, theres no need to wonder whether he wants you or not, a boy doesn't cry as he did for nothing. Isn't it strange you've been going with Ken such a time, and yet you cannot make up your mind, while I only saw Billy for two days, and I'm afraid we both fell with a bump, and honestly duckie its going to last. I suppose that sounds a bit conceited on my part, but I trust Billy completely, and I think he does me.

I'm sorry I couldn't see more of you Ivy, but you did understand how it was, didn't you. I seem to get such little time when I do come, and of course (now that I have new situations to meet)?

I like both the in-laws very much indeed, and I wasn't a bit nervous when once I was inside, but at the gate I will admit that my knees played "Annie Laurie".

Cheerio duck, write soon to me, I need lots of cheering up and tell me all the news.

Lots of love from your old pal.

Dorrie

The letter from Dorrie demonstrates that all was not going smoothly at this time between Ivy and Ken.

Dorrie was an old pal of Ivy's who had moved out of the area. They kept in close contact with one another through letters and visits. From the tone of this letter, and others that were discovered, it appears that Ivy provided the cover for Dorrie to spend weekends back in Birmingham where she pursued her courtship of Billy.

2

Love and War

Ivy and Ken were married on 10 December 1938 at the Methodist Chapel in Aston Lane, Perry Barr, Birmingham. Ken was 26 and Ivy 25. Their wedding reception was held at The Old Crown and Cushion in Perry Barr. It is interesting to note that on the receipt for the wedding buffet an amount of five shillings (25p) has been included for a box of 100 Players' cigarettes!

Ivy and Ken spent only eight months together as a married couple before Ken was called up for active service with the RAF on 24 August 1939. This must have been a terrific blow to them. Ken would not be permanently at home again until November 1945. He was released from service on 11 January 1946.

Ivy and Ken's Wedding, 10 December 1938
Left to right: Rosy, Pop, Kath, Ken, Ivy, Wal, Doll, Charlie, Fanny

Ken's Squadron waiting for orders 1940
Ken is seated on the right-hand side of the bench

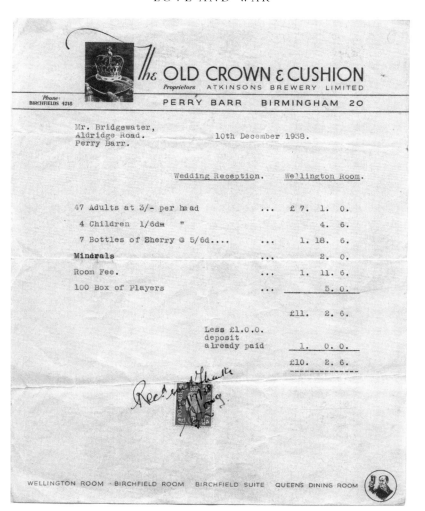

Wedding Reception Account – The Old Crown & Cushion

172 Aldridge Road
17th December 1944

My Dear Ivy,

Well I am very pleased to know you have got over your trouble once more (or is it only just starting). I was really very surprised that it was not a boy after you being so very different all through, but never mind the girls are very nice little girls and fancy having a blonde. I expect it's like Kenneth was. I always told you he had white hair on a pink head so I expect it will go golden as she grows a bit.

Well Ivy don't worry about Linda's reception of her, she quite understands that her Mommy wanted to bring her the very best baby they'd got at the Nursing Home and the really best one is a little Christine sister, so she's quite content. If she does all for it that she says she's going to do you needn't worry you'll have nowt to do with it she's going to Baff her and put her to bed and take her out and do everfinks for her. The only thing that's troubling Linda now is that she <u>knows</u> her Mommy hasn't got any milk in her 'feeds' for little Christine, so she'll have to have some of her "Linda's" dinner. You'll have to watch her or she'll be feeding her.

I'm already longing to see the little duck. I wish you weren't so far off, but never mind the time will soon pass. Linda is very well she's eating well and talking my head off she's got the Williams disease, talking diabetics, she's 12 hours a day non stop. She sleeps 12 hours from 7 to 7 so I can't grumble at that can I and she lets me stop a bit longer while she has her milk and biscuits etc. She still does all the washing up and today she's put the mincemeat in the jars. I've made a bit. When she's gone to bed tonight I'm going to make a few pies and I'll put you a few in.

I don't like to think of you being hungry still you should have a good feed after next Tuesday. I hope Ken will be able to get off to help you home but if he doesn't you just get a taxi and come home in comfort.

I'm afraid I'll have to stop now Linda just won't give me peace so wishing you a happy Xmas and the best of luck and prosperity in the Coming Year and love from Linda and Mom.

Ivy and Ken's wartime babies, 1945
L to R: Muriel, Lorna, Linda

The letter beginning 'My Dear Ivy' is dated 17 December 1944 and was from Rosy. It was sent to Ivy whilst she was in Sorrento Maternity Hospital, arriving the day after Lorna's birth.

There were signs of aggravation between Ivy and Rosy from time to time – and signs that Ken had to intervene and be peacemaker between his mother and his wife.

Rosy was disappointed to hear of the birth of a third grand-daughter and described Lorna's arrival as 'trouble'. She also referred to Lorna as Christine in her letter. I expect she thought it appropriate as the new baby had been born at Christmas. However, Ivy had her way over the choice of name and mollified Grandma by using Christine as a second name!

Grandma had a shock coming to her because Ivy and Ken produced a fourth daughter, Jennifer, in March 1949 – exactly 21 days before Rosy died.

RAF Turweston   21.12.44
Nr Brackley, Bucks

Darling,

I hope you get this letter in time dear, but I think you will.

I called at the Mail Office and fixed up the notice in the "Mail" so your friends will know, all about it.

I felt very miserable when I was at home darling, just because I had got to come away and leave you all by yourself. But you <u>can</u> see the sense of my having <u>all</u> my leave with you, can't you dear, and not wasting it messing about on my own.

I expect you realise now, darling that I love you more than ever. You know that because I came to see you, when I said I wouldn't. It was entirely impromptu, as I really had made my mind up not to come in the afternoon, but I just couldn't leave you on your own darling.

But I didn't like having to see you in front of other people darling. I did so much want to hold you tight. I think that's why I looked so fed up. I know I did.

I have fixed up my leave OK darling and it is from 28th Dec to 8th Jan – 12 days. But I travel at 12am on 27th Dec, so I shall be home in time to pick you up at 10.30am on 28th.

I shall go out early on 28th and get my own rations, so that should see us thro the first day or two.

We are getting two days off at Christmas – 25th and 26th. Isn't it a pity it can't be tacked onto my leave darling. But it can't, I'm afraid, as it will take them all their time to get my ordinary leave thro, as it is. However it will be two days rest, so I'll just be able to lie in bed and think of you darling.

Linda was going on OK at Mom's and I hear Muriel is as good as gold, and it looks as if they'll have a good Christmas anyway.

Linda absolutely swears and argues that there is <u>no</u> cot for Lorna; at least, she admits that there is a cot, but it isn't a "proper" one, and it <u>definitely hasn't</u> got curtains on it!

Mom had the piano tuner (Oh, I remember I told you this).

Mom looked after me very well this time, and I really enjoyed being there for a change. She really is pleased about this baby now dear, and does she love your children? Honestly darling she thinks the world of 'em, and she's just dying to see Lorna.

Well darling, I don't know how I'll wait until I see you. I do so much want to be with you.

But we'll have 12 whole days together darling and I'll be able to hold you tight, although I shan't be able to "<u>hold</u>" you. But I'm not worried about that dear, so long as I can just be with you.

Another load of coal has come dear, and it is real Christmas coal. Burns a treat. I have asked Doll to put the electric fire on for an hour daily to keep the place aired, as it seemed very damp darling. But I'll have a nice fire for you when you come home dear.

I have decided to drop a line to your Mom and Co, as I think they will like to hear all the news. I expect I'll write to Jess and Jack as well.

I am not a bit upset about it being a girl now dear. In fact now I've had time to think it over, I realise that it doesn't really make any difference. We shall lose 'em anyway at some time to come. But I'm afraid they'd better learn some of the old man's tricks. I can't stand women that don't understand their own cars, etc. anyway.

I suppose I shall have to concentrate on Doll's houses instead of Hornby trains etc. Roll on peacetime, I'll soon make 'em some toys then. And if this war goes on, believe me, I'll be prepared for next Christmas. In fact I intend to start looking for material right now.

Well, darling, I think this is about all for today. Now don't you get being fed up dear, because it is only 6 days now, and you'll be in my arms again.

Remember that I love you more and more. I really do darling. All I want is to be home with you always darling.

So keep your pecker up dear. I'll write as much as I can.

Always your own

Loving

Ken

PS I thought you looked the rosiest in the ward.

Love

Ken

Ken's letters to Ivy began to flow in great numbers once he was posted to Italy. From the time of his call-up in 1939 to the time of his first airmail letter home in 1944, Ivy had given birth to three baby girls – Linda in 1940, Muriel in 1942 and Lorna in 1944.

The letter of 21 December 1944 was sent to Ivy in the Sorrento Maternity Hospital in Birmingham at the time of Lorna's birth (16 December 1944).

Jess was Ivy's eldest sister and Jack was her husband.

It seems that, initially, a third daughter was not thought to be a wonderful thing either by mother-in-law Rosy or by Ken. However, it is crystal clear that these feelings faded immediately they set eyes on the baby.

Ken did teach all his daughters to change their own wheels on bikes and cars, to mix and use concrete, to wallpaper and paint, to change fuses and to tend the garden. He had little time for girlie girls.

Rosy (Ken's Mother) with Linda

RAF Turweston   23/12/44
Nr Brackley, Bucks

Darling

I don't know if you have written to me dear, but I am really hoping to get a line. However, if you haven't already written it won't be any good now really, as I start for home on 27th at 12am.

How are you now, my dear, you should be getting on fine now? And how is Lorna progressing?

I made enquiries about a taxi, but Bunting can't provide one, and Warwick Hire will cost about 25/-, so I hope you really can manage on the 'bus.

There will only be a little walk at this end, won't there.

We are now getting two and a half days at Christmas, but there has got to be a skeleton duty crew on, so I have volunteered to do it from 12am Sat till 8am Sunday. That then puts me clear for the two days. Of course there's really nothing to do. We've just got to stand by in case any visiting aircraft come in.

I have made another brooch, and it really is a wizard job. It took me 45 minutes this time. So perhaps I'll make a bob or two out of it after all.

I have been talking to a bloke from India, and he says when his people sent out fags, he used to actually receive one parcel out of four, on average. So it looks like waste doesn't it?

We are having a very slack time here. It is foggy every day, with no flying, and consequently no work to do. So we are packing up at 3pm each day which is a very nice change.

Well darling I hope you'll get this on Christmas Eve, and then ther'll only be 4 days to wait won't there. I am so much looking forward to holding you in my arms again darling.

We'll have a fire in the bedroom, and it will be lovely won't it darling: I really am looking forward to this leave darling, and I just hope that

Lorna will let us enjoy it, don't you. She seemed contented enough to me dear.

Must close now. A long one tomorrow.

All my love dear, Your Own

Ken xxx

Considering that Ivy was in hospital having just given birth to a third daughter, this letter seems a little impatient. However, it shows how very important Ivy's letters were to Ken – a virtual lifeline in troubled times.

Bunting was the local garage – just a stone's throw from Rosy's house at 172 Aldridge Road. It is hard to imagine Ivy leaving hospital with a newborn, in the dead of winter, to travel home by bus, with just 'a little walk this end'.

Ken made lovely wax brooches. Several different colours of sealing wax were melted and swirled together onto little shaped cards. Tiny brass safety pins were fastened to the back. He continued to make brooches long after the war was over to supplement their income.

DARLING

MAKE UP YOUR MIND <u>QUICKLY</u>. A TAXI WILL BE
OUTSIDE AT <u>10.15 am</u>. HE CANNOT WAIT.
ROSY WANTS YOU TO GO TO 172 TO STAY <u>ONE</u> OR
<u>TWO</u> NIGHTS ONLY.
SHE HAS LOADS OF GRUB WHICH MUST BE EATEN
INCLUDING A 9lb TURKEY (STILL RAW), CAKE, PORK,
CHICKEN AND GOD WOT!!!
SHE SUGGESTS YOU WOULD DO BETTER TO BE
"HELPED" A BIT FOR A COUPLE OF DAYS IN AN AIRED
HOUSE AND BED.
OUR HOUSE IS COLD. THE CUPBOARD IS BARE! I
AGREE.
IT WILL GIVE ME A COUPLE OF DAYS TO GET THE
GRUB IN.
IT WILL PLEASE HER, AND SHE'S A BIT TIRED OF
LINDA NOW.
ALSO LINDA NOW CRIES FOR MOMMY.
MUST TELL DRIVER WHERE TO GO.
I LOVE YOU.   KEN

Rosy is determined to be 'helpful'. Ivy is not keen on leaving
hospital with the new baby and spending Christmas with
Rosy. Ken seems to be caught between the two. Suggesting
that Linda was crying for her Mommy probably did the trick.
The fact that Ken wrote the whole of this note in capitals,
with much underlining and concluding with 'I LOVE YOU',
shows both his frustration and his effort to be peacemaker
between his wife and his mother.

DARLING.

    MAKE UP YOUR MIND
QUICKLY.   A TAXI WILL
BE OUTSIDE AT 10.15 AM.
HE CANNOT WAIT.

    ROSY WANTS YOU
TO GO TO 172 TO STAY
ONE OR TWO NIGHTS. ONLY.

    SHE HAS LOADS
OF GRUB WHICH MUST
BE EATEN. INCLUDING A
9 lb TURKEY (STILL RAW)
CAKE, PORK, CHICKEN AND
GOD WOT.!!

    SHE SUGGESTS YOU
WOULD DO BETTER TO
BE "HELPED" A BIT FOR
A COUPLE OF DAYS IN
(OVER)

AN AIRED HOUSE AND
BED.

    OUR HOUSE IS COLD.
THE CUPBOARD'S BARE.'

    I AGREE.

    IT WILL GIVE ME A
COUPLE OF DAYS TO
GET THE GRUB IN.

    IT WILL PLEASE
HER, AND SHE'S A BIT
TIRED OF LINDA NOW.
ALSO LINDA NOW CRIES
FOR MOMMY.

    MUST TELL DRIVER
WHERE TO GO.

    I LOVE YOU.

    KEN -

Ken's abrupt note to Ivy in Sorrento Maternity Hospital

December 1944
Wednesday

My Dear

I am jammed like a sardine aboard T.S.S. Dinard and I am being overlooked. We went aboard at 7.30am and sailed at 9.30am from Dieppe to Newhaven. We expect to arrive in three and a half hours.

A telegram should have arrived on Wed for you.

We proceed to Hednesford and I expect to get home by Saturday. But that is optimistic darling. It may be Sun or Monday. However, be prepared.

Impos to write more under the prevailing conditions.

All my Love

Ken x

PS If it gets near the nibs bedtime <u>don't</u> keep them up. I would rather have the chance to "prepare" their presents. There are some things that might want pressing a bit before they see 'em.

PPS Don't know that I want Rosy around either, so steer her off somehow. But don't upset her or yourself over it.

It is endearing that Ken wanted to prepare the 'nibs' (children's) presents in secret. The presents were probably clothes that had got crushed in his kitbag.

Once again, the difficulty with Rosy is mentioned.

31

On Active Service   20.4.45 (3)
A.P.O. 8340

My Darling

This is just another line in case No.2. goes astray. We are now on the 4th day out, and I am still enjoying it immensely.

It isn't quite so warm today, but I expect another couple of days will see us getting into Tropical Kit.

Save all my letters up darling as some of them may be of interest later on. I am hoping that there will be some waiting for me at the other end darling, as your air mails should have beaten the boat.

I wish you could see this cabin packed with hammocks at night! It really is a scream. Something like sardines in a tin you know. But I don't go much on a hammock. I tried it first night and woke up all of a bunch, and have since slept on the floor which I find much better.

I get about 9 hours sleep each night, and still enjoy a kip on the deck in the daytime.

We have got an excellent Bridge school going, and we have some real good fun at it. Funnily enough, there is very little bridge played aboard, and it's amazing how many watchers gather around.

The water has got much rougher this last two days, and a lot of the lads are very fed up indeed.

Everything is very cheap on board. A Nylon toothbrush 1/- and 200 Players for 5/6d!! And half a pound of sweets costs 7d or so.

I know I've told you most of this before, but it's just in case the first one goes astray. Anyway darling, I am having a good time, and I have every confidence of reaching my destination safely. This sailing isn't quite like it is on the pictures you know dear!

Look after yourself my darling, and the children and give my love to all.

We are all veterans here darling, so I expect we'll be home for Christmas and the first year we can we'll go and stay at the Lindens again at Llandrindod Wells.

All my Love my

Own darling

Yours

Ken xxxx

L.L.&M. xxx

Ken started numbering his letters so that it would be obvious if any went astray. As it happened several did. They may have been held back by the censor or just lost on their complicated journey from the front.

Both Ivy and Ken were enthusiastic bridge players and it formed the entertainment for many Saturday nights with friends and family, together with evenings of whist, dominoes and chess.

Ken always added a kiss (*LL&M xxx*) at the end of his war letters for 'the nibs'. Jennifer had not yet arrived.

Darling,

Just a hurried note to let you know we've arrived safely. I have very little time to write much, and I don't know just how much I can say either.

It is amazing to think that even Linda knew where Daddy was.

The most delightful surprise of all, was to find your <u>two</u> letters awaiting me. I will reply to them in my next.

Don't have any worries darling, as I'm quite OK except that my feet still play hell. The M.O. who passed me grade 1 was mad!

No darling, I have no regrets, and the fact that I gave up my commission for this trip doesn't mean a thing.

At least it means that I am parted from you darling, but absence only makes one fonder. That's impossible in our case of course dear, as you know, I just live for you, and for the day.

And this trip will just be a mine of knowledge to impart to you and the children on those <u>lovely</u> <u>cold</u> winter evenings to come.

All my love darling to you and the children – always.

Your Own

Loving

Ken xx

L.L.&M. xxx

C/o R.A.F.   27 April 45   (5)
A.P.O 8340

My Darling

Well, here we are again dear. Everything in the garden is still lovely. We haven't reached our final destination yet but we have managed to visit Naples and the ruins of Pompeii en route, so we are seeing a bit of the world after all. I wanted to see lots of other things really, but of course there wasn't time.

If I should want any money any time send it registered but I don't think I shall really. However, if I ever <u>do</u> want any, I'll ask for it, but I'm inclined to think the boot will be on the other foot really.

Don't expect me to buy or send any presents home. A pair of shoes for you (worth about 10/- to 12/-) cost 3000 lira = £7.10.0. !!!! A loaf costs 50 lira = 2/6d. Fags are <u>unobtainable</u> in shops. But so far, they are issuing us with enough so <u>don't</u> send any.

It was just marvellous to receive your two letters darling. They came in <u>two to three</u> days!!! But I expect mine will take longer due to censorship.

I am glad you had a good journey, and pleased you got plenty of help. Yes, darling it was a struggle to get to see you sometimes, but it was well worth it.

Sorry to hear the nibs have whooping cough, but I expect they'll soon get well again in your care.

When I am finally settled I will send you a nice long letter darling, but at the moment you must realise I am still on the move, and it is never safe to unpack much gear, as off we go again at a minutes notice.

Don't forget that I love you tons and tons dear and am just waiting until we can be together again always and always. Give my regards to all darling.

All my love darling,

Always your own

Ken xxx

LL&M xxx

Blackpool

My Darling

Well, this is one hell of a life so far. We are just living like gentlemen. We had one parade this a.m. and were dismissed at 10.30. Paraded again at 2.45, and am now back at the digs after the most painful inoc I've ever had. Boy what a stinger! But I understand it has this immediate effect and no afters. It's OK now, at all events.

Things are looking up! It now looks as if there's a good chance of a "36" so look out for your husband on Saturday – I dearly hope ???

We are making the best of things here and trying to have a good time. Last night we went to the Grand Theatre to see "The Last of Mrs Cheyney". It was damn good indeed. We went in the "Gods" and paid 1/6d. Don't be jealous darling. I wish you were here to go with me. Tonight we are going to see the Arthur Askey show. I have included the programmes.

Had a nice haircut this afternoon. Cheers! It looks as if almost anything can be bought here so if I come home, I'll probably bring some nice crockery.

The digs are very nice, and we have a wash bowl in the room, with a bathroom next door. I have now moved into a proper bed, so should get a good sleep tonight. The weather has now turned good again, although there's a good breeze on the front.

This is all for now darling.

All my Love

Always Your Own

Loving

L.L.&M. xxx   Ken xxx

R.A.F. Blackpool

April 1945
Friday

Darling

Well dear we certainly are having some fun. It is all very interesting and we're having bags of time to ourselves.

The digs are marvellous and the landlady quite nice. In fact it is like the place we stayed at in 1937 as anything. Do you remember the "Lindens" at Llandrindod Wells? Of course we aren't paying anything so we can't grumble if it don't pan out quite as well can we?

I am meeting a lot of the old gang on this draft, and quite a crowd from 32 M.U. are here. I've also met my "confederate". The first thing he asked me was "Have you got 'em with you?" That was Tommy Parry, who used to share the Bank with me!

We enjoyed the Arthur Askey programme last night. It was really good.

The position re a "36" is still the same, so I still don't know if I'm coming or not, so please darling, don't bank on it, and then you won't be disappointed.

Lettuces are 5d. here, and fish abounds, but other things seem to be dear. You can certainly buy almost <u>anything</u> – at a price!

Don't forget to send me Kath's address, as I must write to her sometime.

The cakes in the shops here are just like pre-war at home. Again <u>if</u> I come I'll try and bring some, as I'm sure our nibs haven't seen any like 'em.

I could use a supply of <u>hard</u> sweets darling. I feel that I really could rob the kids for once dear. It will be nice to suck a sweet now and then, on the boat. If you can manage it, send 'em in <u>tins</u>. There are some Players 50 tins under the yellow sheet in the pink toy box. I can use them anyway for keeping fags in.

I can't think of 'owt else now darling, except that I haven't been tempted to desert you yet, although they're waiting on every street corner at 2d. a bunch. Most of the blokes are fixed up already! I'm only paying one halfpenny for my buns.

All my love darling,

Always Your Own

Ken xxx

L.L.&M. xxx

Kath (Ken's sister) in her Red Cross uniform

Kath was Ken's older sister. She served in the American Red Cross during the war and sent food parcels to Ivy and the children whenever it was possible. Relationships between

Kath and Ken were strained due to an unexplained family falling-out*. They did keep up a limited correspondence, but there were only very rare face-to-face meetings between the two.

The third paragraph of this letter is a bit of a mystery. We don't know what M.U. stands for – nor who Ken's 'confederate' (Tommy Parry) was and what he means by 'who used to share the Bank with me'.

* See *Flying off the Shed Roof*

Kath meeting with Eleanor Roosevelt at Hitler's Bunker

R.A.F. Blackpool

April 1945
Thursday

My Own Darling

This is it! From now on I cannot tell you much, in the interests of security, so you must grin and bear it. Your letters will be subject to censor on the way in, and mine may be, at G.P.O.

Had a pleasant journey up and two of us played cards with two M.O. Health Office dames on the train. This killed the 5 hours nicely, and they also fed us on egg sandwiches, which was a good thing, as Turweston gave us no grub.

It was a lovely warm day and the officials here seem to be very decent. We only carried our kit 100 yards, and then got transport. We are all in civvy digs. 10 in ours. 100 yards from the sea. It is damn cold today. I sent my shoes home, hope you got 'em OK. Please send on my swimming trunks. I forgot 'em. They are under the yellow sheet in the back room in a cube shaped cardboard box. I think that is the only thing I forgot dear. This is naturally a bit disjointed. The grub is fairly good in our house, but the lady is new to the game, and doesn't really know how to feed men. We had to tell her that eighth inch slices of bread and butter were no good to us or her. Keep that money towards your birthday dear. I shall be sending more money on in the future I expect, so when I do, use what you need, and then put the balance in the bank for "us" when I come home again.

I didn't sleep last night darling. I just lay awake until 4am thinking of you. I hate to say this darling, but I don't think you'll see me again.

Passes and leave are definitely taboo, as we're likely to jump off any time at all. Keep your pecker up dear, and remember that I am saving myself for you, and that I love you more and more than ever.

I seem to have found a mate already who doesn't drink – thank God – but he smokes! Fate has just cast us into a twin bed together.

All my love dear and another letter tonight.

Your Own

Ken X

L.L.&M. xxx

Ken was a life-long hater of drink, especially beer – but a very committed smoker: twin themes that run through much of his correspondence.

Ken in RAF uniform, 1945

My Darling

It is quite a few days now, since I heard from you, so I am hoping ther'll be a letter today. Had a day off yesterday, and went into Foggia. There isn't much there, really, and nothing to do. A 35/- camera costs about £40.00. A pair of 2/6d. sun specs cost about 2800 lire, (or £7.0.0.), so I shan't be buying any souvenirs. There don't seem to be any food shops, so I don't know what the people eat.

I did buy one little thing, but it was thro' the W.V.S. so the price was reasonable.

A local Iti barber has re-set my razors for me for 20 fags, and they're absolutely whizzo now. We also took some laundry to a local farm house, and were very amused at the flat irons. They are about 6 inches deep, and have a coke fire inside them to keep them hot. As the iron cools off they have to stoke it up.

Had quite an interesting letter from Arthur Bourne (Editor of "Motorcycles") today. He states that he intends to publish my article, and send you the cheque, and a copy of the issue. Please, keep it for me. But more important still, he has made me a tentative offer of a job on the staff for after the war. You know, motorcycle reporter on racing, trials, etc. At any rate, he has asked me to send particulars of my life history, which he says, he will give his careful consideration. This is the job I always wanted darling. So I'm going to really go all out for it.

The weather is still beautiful here, and there is little work really, as the position of the war is changing so rapidly. If only you were here, and the old bike, I could just imagine it to be a holiday camp.

I wrote to Percy and Lil yesterday and said what you asked. Don't forget to send Wal's address, will you dear.

I think this is just about all for now darling. It is only short, so that I can catch the post.

All my love to you and the children

Always your own Loving Ken x

LL&M xxx

Ken used cut-throat razors, which he normally sharpened on a leather razor strop. He was still using this method of shaving long after the war ended. His girls remember the strop vividly. It lived on a hook on the pantry door and if they misbehaved they would be threatened with it. It was an idle threat however, and never actually used.

Ken absolutely loved bikes and cars. He wrote, and had published, many articles for *Autocar* and *Motorcycles*. To his great disappointment the longed-for job with Arthur Bourne did not materialise.

The reference about Ken writing to Percy and Lil with Ivy's request is a bit of a mystery. It has been rumoured around the family that Lorna, who was then six months old, might have gone to them, as they had been unable to have children. This seems unlikely as Ivy and Ken adored all their girls. Lil and Percy did eventually adopt a baby daughter, Pamela.

Ken on the Norton, July 1937

An outing to the Clee Hills (Ivy left)

Sunday 6th May 45   (8)

My Darling

Here we are again. Your letters seem to have stopped. I haven't had one now for several days. Please write as much as you can my dear, because it is really all there is to look forward to out here. There is absolutely nothing to do when off duty, except to lounge about all day. Even the local country is too flat and uninteresting to enjoy hiking. And the local burgh is no use to man nor beast! There is a Naafi there, but who the hell wants to go 5 or 6 miles to the Naafi?

It is still terrifically hot in the daytime. I am cherry red now. Tried 10 minutes in the sun yesterday, and believe me, it's quite enough at a time. Mind you, I'm not daft enough to get burnt, but at the same time it is advisable to get the skin tanned gradually, as it then has a greater resistance to mosquitoes. Wish you could see us in our nets at night. We look like a lot of babies, tucked up in our cribs.

Did you understand what I meant about Arthur Stewart?

Hope you have sent on some fags by now darling. The position is acute. The issue is made on a Wednesday here, and when we arrived on the Saturday they said we weren't on the strength until "next week" which meant we'd got to wait 10 days for our issue, and of course that put paid to our reserve supply. We can't even get any off the non-smokers as they can get 100 lire for 20 off the Itis (5/-). So they won't sell 'em to us.

No there wasn't a letter today darling, so again, I'm anxiously awaiting the post tomorrow. I think you should be getting my letters direct now darling, and I am expecting yours to be the same shortly. I understand that they take 6 days from here, and 3 days from you to me.

We have had a fairly busy day today; - Just heard the news. They say they're starting demobbing on July 1st, so it won't be long now darling.

Look after yourself and the children my dear.

All my love to you darling,

Always and always

Your Own Loving

Ken X

L.L.&M. xxx

P.S. Have got 30 envelopes. K.

It is very clear from this letter how important Ivy's letters were to Ken. She must have struggled to find the time to write, and post, the eagerly-awaited daily letters. At this time Ivy was caring for three small daughters aged five, three and one, all with whooping cough.

It is not known who Arthur Stewart was.

3

Anticipation

My Own Darling

Hows this; two in one day. 10 & 11!!

But I must write again my dearest to celebrate the fact that we have just learned that <u>the war is over</u>!! Thank God darling.

Just fancy, they sent us out here and it only took 4 days for Jerry to get the wind up and pack up in Italy!

But of course darling no doubt we shall still be here for several months, but what a difference! There will surely be something to look forward to now.

Oh Boy, shan't we be watching the demob numbers. 19 is mine do you remember.

Understand that Mr Churchill is broadcasting tomorrow (Tuesday). I think we get 3 days off to celebrate. The boys will be having a tot of vino tonight darling. I should just like to have a tot of coffee with you.

Anyway darling, just carry on as I've told you in my other letters, as I'm almost sure to need the things I've asked for.

And if they should? put me back on the boat again before they arrive, well who cares? I'll be in your arms again instead!

Oh darling, it is really wonderful, isn't it? And I haven't any worries, I feel convinced that I'm going to get a job OK.

I am just looking forward eagerly to being with you again my darling, every day, for always and always.

Well darling there is no more news, as this is two letters in two hours, but remember dear that I love you better than ever before.

Save yourself for me dear one, just a little month or two.

Your Own Loving Ken X

LL&Mxxx

⑪ 7th May 45. Cpl. Bracewell. R.
849 138.
231. WING. C.M.G.
R.A.F. — C.M.F.

My own Darling,

How's this; two in one day. 10 & 11. !!

But I must write again, my dearest, just to celebrate the fact that we have just learned that THE WAR IS OVER !! Thank God darling.

Just fancy, they sent us out here, and it only took 8 days for Jerry to get the wind up & pack up in Italy!

But of course darling, no doubt we shall still be here for several months; but what a difference! There will surely be something to look forward to now.

Oh boy, shan't we be

Joyful 'WAR IS OVER' letter: Mr Churchill's victory speech is recalled

watching the demob
numbers. 19 is mine.
Do you remember.

Understand that he
Churchill are broadcasting
tomorrow (Tuesday). I think
we get 3 days off to
celebrate. The boys will
be having a tot of gin
tonight darling. I should
just like to have a tot of
coffee with you.

Anyway darling, just
carry on as I've told you
in my other letters, as
I'm almost sure to need
the things I've asked for.

And if they should?
put me back on the
boat again before they
arrive well who cares?
I'll be in your arms
again instead!

Oh darling, it is

53

My Darling

I have purposely missed one number from the sequence, for your sake. Well, darling, this is the 8th day without a letter, and I am getting a bit concerned about it. Have you been writing my dear?

We still seem to have nowt to do, and have been "standing by" for 3 days but nothing comes along. We haven't had our two days "official" holiday yet, and when we get it we are hoping to visit one or two seaside towns, and have a look at the blue waters of the Adriatic.

It is sweltering hot, and we just wear trunks and pumps and eat, sleep, lounge and read. About 5 mins is enough in the sun, and then we come into the tent again. Everywhere is dry white dust, clouds and clouds of it, a lot worse than the Welsh trials sections. We get parched, and the water isn't fit to drink unless it's boiled, so we have to be satisfied with the tea we get at mealtimes.

Bought my "issue" pint of beer on VE day, but I only drank about a dessert spoonful of the stuff. I don't know how the blokes can drink it. And the wine is just like very sour vinegar. But still blokes get drunk on it!

The nicest thing to do here is to get washed, and we do it as many times a day as our 4 petrol cans of water will last, and when we've finished washing, we just throw the water over one another.

Am hoping you have sent some fags by now darling; that is my very weak point here.

According to the gen we've heard, they're demobbing groups one to 15 on July the 1st, but we never see a paper, so we don't know if it's true or not. Let me know when you read about it.

I bet Linda and Muriel are beginning to realise that "Daddy ain't coming back" aren't they? What do they think about it all? And how is Lorna going on. I hope she didn't get the whooping cough and I hope the others are now better darling.

I have written to Percy and Lil, and Mom and Kath, but have had no replies from any of them. How is Mom going on? Does she get any better at all?

Did you ever get the money for those other brooches darling I wonder?

Now darling, look after yourself and don't worry about me, because I'm going on fine. I wish I was with you all the time darling, but at the same time I wouldn't have missed this trip for a lot. I only wish you could be here darling, in a tent for two; it would be just heaven dear.

I love you such a lot dear, and I want you very much. Do you look forward to my return darling, as much as I do. I am just living for the day darling, but at the moment it is just a bit too far to risk a crafty weekend isn't it? You know that I would if there was half a chance of a kite doing the return trip darling, but it doesn't bear thought, as the chance is very remote.

Oh well, all my love for now darling, and remember that I love you with all my heart.

I am always your own

Loving Ken x

LL&M xxx

Ken stripped off outside his tent in Foggia, 1945

Ivy was really superstitious about the number 13. Ken was obviously well aware of this and therefore missed it out of his letter numbering system.

Ken is, once again, concerned about the lack of letters – even though he later mentions the children and whooping cough.

The mention of his mother, Rosy, indicates that things between her and Ivy were still a bit tricky: 'Does she get any better?'

Fragment – earlier pages missing

. . . and varied. I am now changing from strawberry to brown. Even I am getting that I can stay in the sun just as long as I like with just shorts and pumps on. If you haven't sent the Opedeldoc please don't bother, as I am now sufficiently hardened not to want it. The only urgencies are light bulb and fags. They're my biggest worry I'm afraid.

Things seem to have slacked off here now that the war is over and we're having a very easy time.

One snag about the heat is that shaving soap dries on one's face as fast as it is put on and it's just like shaving dry. I don't go a bundle on this, and it's very painful for the blokes, because they've only been issued with two very doubtful blades since we came here.

It is a good job that I brought plenty of soap, because we only get <u>half</u> a tablet of Lux per week, perhaps. We didn't get any this week as it happens. This is <u>not</u> an indication that I want some.

I very much hope by now, that the children are getting better darling. It has been a long time now hasn't it.

I <u>may</u> be sending some money next week darling. Now have about 2800 lire in credit. But don't worry about it. It takes several weeks to come thro'. I don't know how long I'll be here, but certainly, I shall save more than ever before, as there's literally nothing to buy. We have an orchard behind us, with millions of damsons and figs coming on nicely. <u>If</u> the blokes will leave 'em alone until they're ripe, then I'll try and send some home, tho' they make it very difficult for us, I'm afraid.

Yes, the orders are out and there's no more censorship darling, so you should get my letters fairly rapidly now.

My God darling, this is definitely the hottest day up to now! We are just dripping with sweat now, and I've got to work this afternoon putting an engine in! The fowls even lay their eggs ready boiled now! We now have flying beetles as big as butterflies. They give a hell of a sock when they hit you. Do you remember that one that nearly knocked me off the bike in North Wales once?

I don't really expect a letter from you today darling, but at the same time I shall be thrilled if I do get one.

They say we have siesta soon. That is, work in the a.m. and p.m. and stretch out on the work pit in the afternoon.

I bet there was some celebrating in Brum wasn't there darling. Did you put any flags out, or anything? I wish Pop could have been here to see it, don't you dear? It doesn't seem like 18 months since he went does it darling?

Well my dear one, I think this is about all I've got to tell you today. Remember darling that I love you more and more. I am longing and longing to be in your arms again. Do you miss me as much as I miss you my darling. Never mind dear, it shouldn't be very long now.

All my love my own darling

Always Your Own

Loving husband, Ken x

L.L.&M. xxx

On Active Service   12th May 1945   (17)

My Darling,

Oh my God, the heat darling! Believe me, I kept my shirt on today!!
And I have changed my mind about the opedeldoc – please send
it if obtainable. My forehead and face are just about raw. With
care, I have just enough opedeldoc to last until you send some
on.

I have been working outside today all day, doing an engine change.
We have got to get it finished, so it has messed all our days off up.
Percy went today, and Bert goes tomorrow, and I have got to wait
until Monday, which means we're all cheesed off, because there's no
fun in going out alone, round here.

Well darling, how's things at home now? Is it beginning to look as
if the war is over yet? If it isn't I expect it will be, by the time that I
get home.

Saw a whacking great insect today like a grasshopper, only about
two and a half inches long, and about as thick as a fountain pen. It
jumps or hops a yard at a time. There seems to get more of these
things each day, with the greater heat.

This weather is really marvellous actually. One can get up at 7.30am
and just put on two garments. Shorts and shirt, and be just nice and
comfortable. And it remains warm up till bed time now. In fact the
houses here have <u>no</u> fire places at all, as they're hardly ever needed.
And in one villa that we were in the kitchen range was on the <u>third</u>
floor next to the roof, so that there would be no smell in the house
anywhere.

Well, I'm afraid this isn't much of a letter my darling, but I know
you love to get them anyway don't you?
You see darling, there is just nothing doing in this joint, so there's
very little to write about.

But I love you tons and tons dear, and it's nice to tell you that isn't it darling. Look after yourself my dear, and I hope the children are better dear.

All my love darling,

Always

Your Own Ken x

LL&M xxx

For most of his life Ken had a really uncomfortable skin complaint. His skin would become very dry and flaky and crack open. He found that he could use a solution called opedeldoc with some degree of success.

After the war, as children we remember him standing in front of the kitchen mirror applying liberal amounts of the medication to his forehead, face, neck and arms. Often his legs were affected, too.

The 'whacking great insect' was a locust. Years later, he brought a dead locust home in an old tobacco tin to study. Ken would never miss a hands-on learning experience for his children.

My Own Darling,

To continue; I'm sorry I had to pack up last night, but the lights went out on me.

I don't know if you are interested in all these sordid details of the life these people live, but I think it is worth while seeing these things.

All the people seem to have a goat, or a sheep, or a mule. And it is quite usual to see a sheep tied to a front door post in a busy street. In many cases these animals live in the house with the people. I saw a bloke come out of a front door with a shovel full of goat manure, and just fling it into the middle of the street. All the houses have their balconies, and often in blocks of flats, someone from upstairs will sling a bucket of refuse down. Potato peels, slops etc. The streets absolutely stink, and the pavements are just black with millions of flies. As you walk along, they just rise in swarms like a black cloud.

In Barletta, if I was asked once, I was asked 30 times if I wanted "Bacon and Eggs", "Fig-Fig", "Woman" or "Bunk Up". It just about gets on your nerves.

It seems to be one of those towns where there is a street for everything. There is a Bakers Street, Carpenters, Tinsmiths, Shoemakers, etc. They all have a so called shop, and this is just like a room facing the pavement. The front wall being formed of a shutter. They just raise the shutter, and sell the stuff on the pavement. But all the actual work of making the things is done on the pavement. The tinsmiths were making really wonderful buckets, tin dishes, saucepans, baths, etc. and all out of sheets of corrugated iron, which they first hammer out flat on the pavement. The shoemaker just sits on a stool in the sun making shoes entirely by hand. Of course, in the main, the men do very little work at all. They just lounge in the sun, and sit at street corner cafes, drinking vino, and singing, and listening to the violins and accordions.

It is nothing to see a mule cart going along the road carrying perhaps a huge cask of vino, or a load of garlic or onions, with the man lying fast asleep on top of the load, whilst his wife trudges along behind, barefoot, and carrying a load on her <u>head</u> which would make our coalmen look silly! Little girls like Linda will easily carry two buckets of water, hundreds of yards, from the nearest communal well, but you never see any males doing such work. The women seem to all do lots of washing. They all do it from about 8 to 90! They have a tub about 18 inches high, and a rubbing board fixed at an angle on the side. They keep dipping the garment in the water, and rubbing like hell on the corrugated board. They use no soap, and do no boiling, and yet the cleaner people seem to get the white things – as white as snow. Then they sometimes throw it on the currant bushes to dry, but in the towns, they have no gardens so they hang it on the <u>walls on the street</u>!

They even do ironing in the street, either on ironing boards, or kneeling down on the pavement. Of course it is very warm and these people live most of their lives in the sun, and just go indoors at night to breed. All culinary work is done sat on stools in the street. The grand mothers usually do this, drawing their stoves up into a "canting" circle. The beauty of it is that as they peel and shell, they simply let the rubbish drop on the pavement and there it stops to rot!

At the moment they have just fetched the harvest in, and every family seems to have its own small quota of corn. This is just laid out on the above mentioned filthy pavements and then all the local children jump and play on and in it. Meanwhile the women beat it with sticks, whilst we also help in the threshing by just walking over it. But poppa just sits on a broken chair and basks in the sun and looks on. Or else he's out in the town following us about waiting to pounce on nub ends of fags when we drop 'em. Then they gather up the straw, and sweep up the grain, and pound it and grind it with more stones on the path, and turn it into some kind of flour.

Another method of threshing is to lay out the corn in a circle, and then to leave it to a mule who trots round and round on it.

The cherries are ripe. I saw a cart load come to the market. They are just tipped onto the ground, and then <u>shovelled</u> with spades into boxes, and sold to the various traders who promptly take 'em to stalls on street corners. They absolutely swarm with flies. And then when they get to the spot where they intend to sell 'em, they have the cheek to cover 'em up with muslin, etc., or bits of old lace to "<u>keep the flies off</u>"!!!

Every farm has its well and the water is either drawn up by hand, or by a mule or ox walking round and round again.

The flocks of sheep and goats are not driven like ours, or controlled by dogs. The shepherd just ambles along, and the sheep <u>follow</u> him in echelon formation. If he decides to rest he just lies down to sleep, and the animals do likewise. They don't stray away! He walks in front to avoid the cloud of dust which the animals always make.

The people all seem to have their own quota of sheep's wool. I suppose they weave it, altho' I only saw it hung out to dry after washing.

Down by the docks, I saw 'em weaving rope, made from odds and ends of rope cast up by the sea. Funnily enough, this is the only town where I've seen <u>any</u> work being done <u>at all</u>!

Barletta, 1945 – The Salvation Army Café is arrowed (bottom left corner)

One of the postcards which I sent yesterday I put an arrow. This points to a beautiful café and garden, taken over by the Salvation Army, and there we sit in deck chairs supping ice cream, sandwiches, etc. We are only allowed to get ice cream from official sources, also any beverages etc. And anyway it would be fatal to get any from an unauthorized source.

As you know the roofs are flat here, having a balcony wall round them and every few yards a spout projects to let out the rain. So when it's wet, one has to walk on the road, or else get drowned. They just stick out like this:

I am enclosing a few more photos today. Tell me whether you like these sort of letters or not darling.

I think this is all I can think of for now, so you'll have to wait until I go another ta-ta for the next. Look after yourself my darling, and I hope you got the flowers.

All my love, my very own,

Always, Your Own

Ken xxx

L.L.&M. xxx

My Own Darling

Have had a marvellous day today. Started early and got to Manfredonia at 10.30a.m. We had a good look around the place, which is
quite small, but absolutely runs to form. There was a bit of excitement
in the place as the Yanks had somehow accidentally? bombed a fish-
ing smack and killed 5 Itis. We got a hitch hike in one of the wagons
fetching a corpse back!

Manfredonia, where Ken witnessed the accidental
destruction of a boat by American forces, 1945

Of course, there were the usual offers of "eggs and chips Joe?"
Incidentally, this town is out of Bounds after 11p.m. We then went
to the Malcom Club and had <u>real</u> eggs and chips (2 eggs) and bread
and butter and tea which cost 65 lire. Eggs are very plentiful, but cost
1/3d. each!

I got a few postcards, some of which I'm enclosing.

We then went to the beach, and lazed, sunbathed and swum, in the nude, for several hours. It's a great life isn't it? It's so hot tho' that it's quite a feat to walk across the sand as it is so hot to the feet.

After our swim we had more tea at the club, and then came back to camp to get the ration – Kensitas! And they even added insult to injury, by taking the extra four out of each packet.

I am enclosing a few eucalyptus leaves, tho' Lord knows why you want 'em darling? I just can't imagine. The red ones are the riper, (or ripest) and if you squash one up and smell it, you'll get the odour O.K.

Talk about the "illuminations"! You should see our lights now! One over my bed and one at each end of the tent, and one spare. Also a switch, over my bed. So it's absolutely whizzo now, and we can write and read at night.

When we were on the beach today it was so clear that we could make out Yugoslavia in the distance!

Wrote to D and F yesterday but didn't attempt to describe things here, as I know you've told 'em all about it.

Well darling, this is all for today, look after yourself darling, and god bless you. I hope there will be a letter tomorrow dear.

All my love darling

Your Own

Ken

L.L.&M. xxx

'D' and 'F' stands for Doll and Frank – Ivy's younger sister and her husband.

66

On Active Service
ROME!

Sunday June 10th 45

My Own Darling,

Well, this is it! And at a hurried glance, it would appear to be the Mecca of the World.

We set off at 7 am this morning, and were on the road for twelve and a half hours. The roads, as we got further north (and nearer the latter battle areas) were atrocious! And it was a very tiring trip. I suppose it was about 280 miles. Can you imagine 20 men and kit in Percy's truck cruising 50 all day over 6 days stuff?

However darling, from first quick impressions it was worth it.

Rome Tour, June 1945. Ken is second left, front row

I really don't know where to start telling you about it, anyway, tonight, I'm too tired. But I could never tell you in a letter just what this experience is like. I will do my best of course, although it will probably spread over many letters.

My primary object, at the moment, is just to let you know I've arrived OK.

We have a very full conducted programme mapped out, so I don't know how much time I'll get for writing, but I'll do the best I can darling.

Of course you cannot write to me here, and anyway, I shall be back at 231 by the time you could. And, am I looking forward to reading your accumulated letters next Friday darling? It is going to be a big loss all this week without them.

A good Samaritan (non smoker) gave me his fag ration for the week, so I am fairly well off, afterall in that respect.

Forget your idea of Rest camps darling. This place is just a dream, and your old man is doing all right.

I'll tell you more about it tomorrow

For now darling, all my love, and save yourself for your

Ever Loving

Ken xxx

LL&M xxx

Percy's truck was a suspension-free, ramshackle, open-backed vehicle that he used to collect milk churns from the farms around Lichfield. The full churns were delivered daily to a dairy in Handsworth where the milk was bottled. It certainly would not have been an ideal mode of transport for battle-weary troops and their kit.

On Active Service, Roma   Mond.11th June

My Own Darling

Well dear, Rome just leaves me absolutely speechless with wonder!
Words fail me. I would hardly know how to start and tell you all
about it. It is so wonderful that it has to be seen, to be believed.

   All I can say is; Thank God, it wasn't bombed, either by us, or the
Germans. It would have been sacrilege.

Card presented to Ken by the Pope in June 1945

It has made up my mind to one thing darling, and that is that <u>some</u> <u>day</u>, <u>somehow</u>, I <u>must</u> bring you to see Rome, and I shall never be content until I've done it.

Today, I posted you a card, and it has <u>Papal</u> stamps on it, and will be postmarked in the <u>Vatican</u> <u>City</u>, so treasure it carefully. I am not buying any postcards here, as I am going to get a book of pictures which embraces it all.

Today we visited the Vatican, and Vatican City. We also visited St Peters. We climbed 692 steps to the top! A height of 565 feet, i.e. half as high again as Blackpool's tower. The view from there is incredible.

Having seen these places, I begin to wonder what the other wonders of the world can be like.

And now, I'm going to make you jealous darling. Tomorrow night we go to the Opera! Carmen! And in the morning and afternoon, we are visiting the Pantheon, and the Royal Palace.

We have seen all the original paintings and sculpture work by

Postcard bearing Papal stamps sent to Ivy from Vatican City

Michelangelo and Raphael. The original mosaics and the Sistine Chapel, about each of which one could almost write a book. And there is one wonderful thing. Michelangelo did one piece of sculpture (not particularly famous, and so I can't find a picture) – and he <u>used Linda as his model!!</u> The likeness is amazing! 11.55pm darling.

Night night darling.

All my love,

Always Your Own,

Ken xxx

Ken kept his promise to Ivy and took her to see Rome, as well as many of the other places he had told her about in his letters. In fact, he took Ivy and all their girls on several European Grand Tours.

The family love the reference to Michelangelo using Linda as one of his models. She did, indeed, look cherubic with masses of thick, dark, auburn curls clustering around her pretty face. How the looks belied the nature – her natural exuberance and daredevil nature caused much mayhem in childhood* and a real thirst for adventure in later life.

* See *Flying off the Shed Roof*

On Active Service   Tues. 12 June 1945
Rome

My Own Darling

Another big day today. Just got in at 11p.m. I am still just as amazed and intrigued with Rome. Today I have been optimistic, and taken a guide's address for future reference.

Postcard of the opera house; Ken was much impressed
by the production of Carmen

Today we visited the Pantheon. The San Maria del Maggore (St Mary's Major). Castello Angelo. The Arcibadilies Lateraneuse (St John's). The Coliseum. The Italian Royal Palace and several other places of great interest.

And then we finished up at the Teatro Realle del Opera and saw Carmen. Really darling it was amazing. You can tell Kath that until she's seen opera in Rome, that she's never <u>seen</u> <u>opera</u> <u>at</u> <u>all!</u>

Of course it was all in Italian, but the singing was excellent, and the showmanship was splendid. A huge stage, with real horses, carriages, etc. And the colour! I have <u>never</u> seen anything, anywhere, to equal the blaze of colour from the dresses etc.

The Orchestra comprised 100 players, and was very good.

"Going to <u>the</u> Opera" is the "done" thing in Rome. There is only <u>one</u> opera house in Rome – thus – going to <u>the</u> opera.

Well darling, I have dreams, and have often had ideas of things I wanted to do. But my one dream now, is to bring you to Rome. I don't know how prices will be after the war, or if Cooks will still run tours, but somehow it's just <u>got</u> to be done!

I haven't much time now, but when I return to camp, I will try to tell you more about it. The people here are better than south. Very friendly indeed. Of course the war never came to Rome. But as usual the Yanks spoiled the prices. Highest yet. An underslip <u>only</u> (no knickers) costs 2650 lire – £6.12.6d. Ladies shoes are 6000-9000!!! Half a pound of steak costs 600 lire (30/-).

Well, all for now my darling. Will be able to send you long letter on Saturday onwards.

Always <u>your</u> <u>own</u>

My Love Ken xxx

L.L.&M. xxx

Usual Address

My Own Darling,

Oh dear, we <u>are</u> in a mess! I cannot get any note paper, so I don't know how I'm going to write to you now. You never <u>write</u> the 1oz darling, so you'd better start enclosing a few sheets. I suppose the Naafi <u>may</u> have some sometime.

Incidentally this letter will prove how you waste paper!

Well darling, we started off for Rome last Sunday at 7a.m. and it took us till 7.30p.m. It was very tiring, but as we got further north the country was like Wales only vaster. The roads were on a par with Bwleh-y-Groes Vyrnwy etc. with tortuous climbs, and hairpin bends for mile after mile. It is nothing in the mountains to start climbing up about a 1 in 10 to 1 in 6 gradient and to just keep on going up and up for 10 or 15 miles. And as you look down over the side, it is almost terrifying to see all these bends <u>immediately</u> below you. Of course when you think of Snowdon etc. you must try and imagine mountains here 3 times as high!

We passed thro' Casserta where we stopped for dinner. This is the place where Jerry signed the Surrender. There is a very beautiful Summer Royal Palace there, with a wonderful estate, and lido and fountains there. (Dick W. is stationed there! Lucky dog.)

And then, all the way beyond that, the country was battle scarred. Every building that could cover a soldier had been shelled or bombed. Almost every bridge had been blown across the ravines etc. and we crossed by Bailey bridges. Wrecked tanks, guns, lorries etc. lie about all around and lots of little corners here and there have the little white crosses of German, English and American graves.

And Cassino! My God, talk about the ruins of Pompeii, this was very much worse! Coventry never saw a bomb compared with this!

And the people in the countryside, still cry out for cigarettes, bread and bully.

It is difficult to imagine a country which has just . . .

There is a page missing here.

There were swimming pools, dance rooms, reading, writing and dining rooms etc. We simply sat at the table, and were waited on by Iti waiters who even washed our iron mugs. It was just like a convalescent home.

We had a good time in its outdoor Lido. The pool was a lovely green shade. 18 feet deep with diving boards up to 32 feet high. A better place than I've ever seen in England. We had our own gharry for daytime use, but the camp run a quarter hourly bus service to the city centre.

There is lots to amuse one in Rome.

For instance. There is very little public transport. All the lorries are very ancient and also the one or two buses, which incidentally only do long distance work. Rome, Naples, etc. I imagine that Jerry pinched any vehicle . . .

The remainder of this letter is lost.

In this letter Ken proved to Ivy that she wasted paper by writing a reply to her using all the spaces she had left in her last letter to him. You might well say that she literally had to read between the lines!

It is possible that the pages missing in this letter were used by Ivy to write back to Ken. She, too, would have found difficulty in obtaining enough paper for her almost daily letters.

A gharry was a horse-drawn carriage used in the same way as a taxicab.

My Darling,

Well dear, we had a real good time in Rome. The Naffi there is a store like Lewis's, and it has been turned into a marvellous place, with the usual bands playing, ballroom, cafeteria, lounges, etc. We had tea there when we went to the opera, and we had fresh <u>strawberries, cherries, peaches and cream</u>! And then I had a <u>tumbler</u> full of ice cream which cost me 20 lire (1/-). We also went to La Bolonese (a café subsidised by RAF) where we had a smashing 3 course dinner and sweets for 6d.

Actually dispatched that £15.0.0. today, so let me know how long it takes to arrive darling. I shan't send the next £10 quite as soon as I anticipated, as of course I spent a few pounds in Rome, and then there's my Rodi leave in 3 weeks time. But I think about thirty bob will see me thro Rodi, as there's nowt to do there only rest, and bathe etc.

We have been to the sea yet again today. This is top hole every afternoon.

There is still very strong information that we'll be moving darling, but I'm inclined to think that low group no's will move north whilst youngsters may go further.

Here are a couple of requirements for that next parcel, which took 20 days, by the way.

1. <u>Palmolive</u> shaving soap. It is <u>not</u> urgent, but I don't want to change my brand, as although the sun does not affect any part of my body, my face is always peeling.

2. A drop more glycerine. The stuff you sent was OK but it should be a 50/50 mixture of each, and it is much too dry as it is. I have tried but I cannot get any here. It looks as tho Wilkins put about 5 of Soap Lin to one of glyc.

I am a bit fed up today. No letter since Friday and a blister on each
heel, and a raw toe where a blister has come off. I can hardly walk
about. Otherwise I am OK, and I never have any bother with that
foot now.

Wal hasn't replied to my letter yet, so I am waiting a bit before I
write again. But you might give me his new address in case.

I am missing you a lot now darling, and the only definite gen re
the release, is that 6, 7 & 8's will be out by August 14th, so unless
they speed it up, it don't look so good to me.
Look after yourself my darling,

     I am always

         Your Very Own

           Ken xxx

LL&M xxx

It seems that Ken was again being troubled by his skin
complaint and sent very specific instructions to Ivy about
what he needed. Something simple like a change of soap
would set up a painful reaction, hence the request for Palmo-
live soap – a brand Ken used all his life.

Ivy had the additional task of tackling the local chemist
(Wilkins) about the ratio of ingredients used in the last bottle
of glycerine; it seems he got it wrong. Ivy would have been
rather uncomfortable about questioning a professional, but
no doubt would have done it for the sake of Ken's well-
being.

My Own Darling,

Well, this is it. Read all about it. We awoke bright and early at the crack of dawn, 04.45. And packed up and finally got away from camp at 7.15. From there, to our surprise, they only took us into Foggia to Group H.Q., where we were to get more transport at 8.30. At 9.30, it still hadn't arrived, so we started 'phoning etc., only to find that "there were not any blokes from 231 going to Rodi this week"!!! – Typical! No transport had been arranged! Bert and I had almost decided to hitch-hike to Rome, when we were finally informed that we could have transport at 10.30. This arrived at 10.45, and we set off.

The journey is about 80 miles over the mountains on a typical Abergwesyn-Tregaran type of road! Absolute hell in a truck! And clouds of white dust. But we got along very well, until we were just in the middle of the narrowest street in a mountain town of Aricana, when the front tyre burst. Of course there was no spare wheel! And no puncture outfit! Again, typical R.A.F. procedure! However, after a time we managed to find a garage(?) and were compelled to repair with <u>cycle</u> patches and hope for the best. We were lucky to complete the journey by 2p.m. The scenery in this part of the country is just like Llanberis or Glencoe, with huge inland lakes thrown in. (And stinking villages too!) For many miles we travelled between hundreds of plum, apple, pear, nut trees etc. Just growing on the roadside for anyone to pick.

Of course the fact that this rest camp is at Rodi means that it isn't at Rodi at all. It is 4 miles away! Again typical of the R.A.F.

The camp consists of a naval training barracks (built in the shape of a ship) on the top of a 300 foot cliff. And there is one house about 200 yards away.

We have our meals on the balcony and look straight down onto a golden beach, with the most marvellous glass like water I have ever seen. It is picture postcard here. The camp itself is not a patch on Rome. It merely comprises of 2 dormitories, dining room, bar and ablutions. There are no amenities at all. So I am writing this letter now at 10p.m. in the dining room. In one corner is the bar (fully crowded) whilst at the same time blokes are playing darts, skittles, table tennis, piano, cards etc!

They gave us a meal when we got here. Bully, tomatoes and onions and peaches. And then we decided on a swim. It is marvellous. 12 blokes had just about a mile of beach all to ourselves! (There are only about 60 blokes here.) There is a raft about 300 yards out. You can walk 200 yards up to your neck and then you've got to swim the rest. Of course I can do it easily, but the job was to get Bert out there as I've only just taught him to swim.

Anyway, he decided to try it, and managed to do about 80 yards and then I had to "rescue" him for the other 20 yards. Well we had lots of fun on and around the raft (water about 10 feet deep there). And then Bert had got to get back to shore again!

We decided that it was best for me to take him the first 30 yards or so, and then for him to swim the rest. So off we went. Then of course naturally, as I was swimming towards the shore I had no idea when I had reached his "depth". And of course with a non swimmer in tow, I couldn't just try where the bottom was, so I just kept going. And when I finally decided to stop, I found that the water was only <u>waist</u> <u>deep</u> and I had "rescued" him about 250 yards! And he is 12 stone!

I really am getting to be a wizard swimmer now. There is another raft <u>along</u> the beach lower down, and I am going to try and swim from one to the other tomorrow. It is 600 yards. And if I can do that, I shall try the return trip another day which will be nearly the mile. But remember darling it is <u>along</u> the beach, not <u>out</u> from the beach.

After that we got some library books, had tea, and then shaved, then had dinner, and finally went to see the district. This took us about 10 mins! And now here I am back again writing to you.

So you see darling, your idea of a rest camp was entirely wrong. There is absolutely <u>nothing</u> to do but rest, lounge, swim, sunbathe etc. There is nothing female for miles, unless it is mountain goats.

The cliffs are steep like Clovelly, and we have to go down about 200 steps to it. This is the most painful part of the holiday.

Anyway it will be very enjoyable in one way. But I wish you were here on these wonderful sands. It would be a marvellous place for a honeymoon. And I think the kids would love this water and sand. It's almost indescribable. The water is crystal clear down under, a marvellous blue, and as still as a bowl of water in the sink. The damn wireless has started now.

We shall probably have a look at Rodi tomorrow, but we don't know yet as we are tied by meal and transport times. And we are not going to walk that 4 miles as it is all up and down, and hairpin bends like the Lynton and Lynmouth area.

Rodi, 1945 – where Ken spent time at a 'rest camp'

I realise now darling how much the fags mean, because we came away without this weeks ration, and they don't issue 'em here until Thursday. But I've got 200 of yours with me darling, so I'm all right.

I love you so much darling, and I'm going to miss your letters this week.

Always your very own

With all my Love

Ken xxx

L.L.M. xxx

Rodi   Wednesday 11th July 1945

My Own Darling,

Here we are again. We saw another film last night "It's a pleasure", in Technicolour, it was quite good indeed.

This morning I had the Adriatic all to myself at 6am and at that time it was hot enough for sunbathing! The water was just like a sheet of glass. There wasn't a ripple on it, and when standing on the raft you could see everything on the bottom at 20 feet. And when I was swimming under water today the fishes were swimming round me. You can look up from under water and see the sun shining, and bubbles and all the colours imaginable.

It would be marvellous to have a holiday with the children here. They could just wear their Birthday suits all day long, as the Iti children do, and it would be a real holiday as there's <u>nothing</u> else to do.

Bacon, eggs and tomatoes for brecker today, but tiffin was lousy.

Bought some more Oranges today. 10 for 20 fags and half pint of fresh olive oil for 7 fags. So have anointed myself all over with it. My skin must have been dry, for it soaked straight in.

We went swimming again after breakfast and again after tiffin.

Old Bert is getting almost expert now, and can swim under water too.

We are just having our afternoon cup of tea, after which we'll probably go swimming for a change.

I am enclosing 3 cuttings. The Russian one makes you think doesn't it? It would mean £1200 to me! The German one is just for interest, and the picture of the girl, I leave you to guess why I cut it out. See if it strikes you as it struck me?

These Itis amuse me. They all swim, and many of them have no costumes so they go in in anything. There are 3 women come here every day. Two about 45 (your build) and one about 55-60 (Our

Rosy's figure). The two younger ones wear pre-1914 war costumes (you know, long legs, and arms and stripes around them) and the big older dame wears a daring brassier and trunks! How the brassier holds out under the strain, I don't know!

Other women will strip to vest and knickers, whilst others just barge in <u>fully dressed</u>! And when they come out they just walk away saturated and let the clothes dry on 'em. The men generally go in in their trousers or naked. They just don't care a damn. And nobody takes any notice at all.

This is all the news ? for now darling.

All my love always

Your Own Ken xxx

LL&M xxx

PS I wish you were here!

The three cuttings are something of a mystery. It seems the Russian one was a job offer for after the war. The German one 'is just for interest' and we know nothing more – and the picture of the girl must surely have reminded Ken of one of his children, probably Linda.

Usual Address   Monday July 16th 1945

My Own Darling

Well dear, the news is great, isn't it? You can really start to count the days now darling, because I reckon if I come home by sea, that I shall only be here for another 8 weeks! Group 18 will be cleared out by 30th Sept, so I should be out myself by Oct 14th.

I didn't write to you on Sat, because we had "rumours" of this news, and I felt that I just couldn't write until I'd confirmed it, back here. Anyway it's quite true darling.

You had better get hold of Fred sometime, and find out how he's fixed. See whether he will be ready to start back in the old job pretty soon, because I really think that any ancillary trade to the Building will see us thro' until retirement age. And also, I do really want to work for No 1 if pos.

Of course I intended to write this yesterday, but oh what a journey we had. First the driver was a novice, who seemed frightened of that mountain road. So much so that before we'd done 10 miles, we all had the wind up, and after about 15 miles, we crashed into a mule cart. I agree that the "driver" of the cart was stretched out upon it <u>fast asleep</u> and that it was on the wrong side of the road, but at the same time any <u>normal</u> driver could have missed it. However, we flung the remains of the cart into the ditch and carried on. And then the motor began to misfire, finally conking out altogether.

The driver just stood and gaped at it, whilst the lads started tearing it apart! After about 3 hours we gave up, and Bert and I decided to hitch hike. I stopped a truck and the bloke said he'd take us, so we all piled aboard. And then the driver of this truck decided to have a look at ours.

I suggested that it was a waste of time, and that he'd do better to tow us, but no, he only spent another 3 hours messing about, and

An overloaded ox cart in Italy, similar to the one that Ken's
squadron accidentally ran off the road

finally towed us 50 miles or so. Of course the weather was the normal
100 degrees or so, and we had neither food nor drink, so after taking
all day for a 3 hour trip, I felt pretty grim last night.

And I didn't like the 5.30a.m. touch much, this morning either!

I haven't got your letter by me now, as I'm writing this at "work"
but the 500 fags which you dispatched on 6th June, arrived on 10th
July, so they took between 4 and 5 weeks. I have also received 4 x
200's, so as you previously stated that you had dispatched 8 lots, I
should receive fags each week now until August 15th approx.

That will exhaust your original orders. And the final order I asked
you to send should then see me thro' until Sept 15th, and then I don't
think I'll be troubling you any more dear. So if you have sent that
600 I asked about, don't send any more now.

If I have come unstuck in my estimate, then that's just too bad.
But I shall conserve a reserve out of the present 900 in my possession.
And I am taking over any fags that come thro' for Bert, as it looks as
if he'll be off home in 3 or 4 weeks – Group 16!

Incidentally, my holiday at Rodi panned out very well, and didn't
really cost me much, at all.

A bit more news: Bert has gone for his medical this afternoon, so it won't be long now dear.

The weather is still terribly hot here. A lot hotter than at Rodi.

Funny thing, darling, but I began to get terribly homesick last week darling. I suppose it was due to the lack of letters from you, and the lack of demob news. I miss you such a lot darling, and altho' I was on holiday, I was very fed up, and had lots of time to think of how far away you are.

But the news seems to have just come along in time to buck me up darling. I can hardly wait for your first letter when you know the news. But I expect you have already seen it in the papers, haven't you, darling? It's very funny darling, but do you realize that I <u>might</u> be able to undo those parcels that I sent you myself! According to all I hear, I might easily get there first.

I am hoping very much to get to Sorrento before I return darling, because they have got some presents really worth while there. So I hope to get there if it's only for an hour or two.

I was very thrilled to find your nice long letter waiting for me darling, last night, and now that I am back in the tent I can answer it. You timed it just right dear. It arrived on Sunday. I should have been very disappointed had it not been here.

I cannot make too much of Linda's drawings, altho' I can see she has got some idea of faces. But tell her that Daddy says it's very good indeed.

I can't say how pleased I am to get a letter from Stan Bradley. But I think you know as well as I do, how much I wanted his address. Sounds as if he intends to stay in the mob doesn't it? But he was always very keen, I know.

If you sent a parcel on June 30th it should arrive any time this month, but I shouldn't send any more now darling. Anything I'm short of now, I'll just have to do without until I get some. – And I'm sure I can manage that long – (short) I mean, darling.

Very glad you liked the photo. I can't understand where the Vatican postcards have got to unless they went by sea. Kath's was addressed to "172".

I am not a bit envious of Dick. After all darling, it was <u>never</u> any use making it anything to worry about was it? And so long as we are happy, it doesn't matter.

I think the holiday charge is disgusting. Especially re Linda and Lorna. (Why charge for Lorna at all?) anyway darling I still leave it to you. All the same it's just struck me. I wonder what the lady at 6 Crystal Road, South Shore would charge? I forget her name. It may be worth while, you know.

Well darling, it's just too exciting looking forward to coming home again, and to think that we shall be together always and always.

I intend to see Arthur Bourne in London, re a job, and failing that I'd like to form a partnership with Fred. I really don't want to go to Armstrongs (who are duty bound to take me) as the wages will be too low. I don't know how the wages are at home now, but I want a decent one to keep us on, don't I.

The "Motorcycle" job would sure to be about £400 a year plus expenses otherwise the painting stunt as the best bet.

The breeze is blowing thro' this tent at the moment, just like wafts of hot air from the oven on a Sunday! It's just about unbearable.

Oh well, darling, get that mixed grill ready. 2 eggs, chips, tomatoes and liver and onions and a huge pot of tea. My estimate is that there's

89 days to go!

Always your very own, Loving

Ken xxx

L.L.&M. xxx

Fred was a painter and decorator, married to Ivy's elder sister, Violet. Ken had worked occasionally with Fred before the war and it seems he meant to do so again once the war was over. It is amazing that he thought it would see them through to retirement age. Ken was about 33 when he wrote this – a long, long way off the official retirement age of 65.

It is a good thing that Ivy was brilliant at mental arithmetic. The situation with the 'fag rations' certainly takes some working out.

Usual address

My Own Darling

I have just been having a nice wash and shave, and I was thinking a lot about you, so I had a particularly careful shave for you darling. And I have a tablet of Yankee "Cathay" Soap, and so now I smell lovely, and I'm lovely and soft. Which reminds me. Please get that fire stoked up because I want a marvellous bath just for you when I come home.

They are beginning to introduce lots of bull here now that there's very little to do, and the boys are very fed up about it. Of course we are a bit more used to that sort of thing.

I can't understand that parcel racket. Your last was dispatched on 25th June, and has not arrived, whilst a parcel came for Bert today dispatched on the 11th July! 16 days! His was registered, and cost 1/6d. for quite a large parcel. However, I expect mine will arrive shortly, and then it won't matter darling any more, because I have asked you not to send again.

We have had a nice quiet time this week with Bert away. At the moment Jock is on guard, and Percy and I are here just on our own. Bert comes back tomorrow, and we ain't looking forward to it very much.

For a change it is a lovely cool evening, but it has been hot all day with lots of "sand devils" about.

I said it was nice and quiet, but Jock and his mate have just walked in, and it looks like as if they intend to do their "guard" in the tent.

I am missing you a terrible lot now darling, but only in spirit.

Honestly darling, I never think of the "other thing" because I <u>know</u> it is impossible, but just the same, I shall want you very much when I <u>do</u> come home. Never, never yet have I felt like going anywhere else.

I do really love you too much for that darling.

I am just reading Cronins "Stars Look Down". It seems darling that the people that <u>can</u> be faithful to each other are <u>very</u> <u>very</u> few darling. And I do believe in you completely darling, as I know you believe in me.

So much so that I know it's very rarely necessary to mention the matter my dear.

I told the M.O. off before I went to Rodi, when he gave me some advice about V.D.

I told him that I had 3 children at home and asked him if he thought I'd risk their future as well as my own for a tuppenny thrill?

I told him to kindly mind his own affairs, and he didn't like it much.

Always darling

Your Very Own

Loving

Ken xxx

L.L.&M. xxx

My Darling,

I'm afraid I couldn't write yesterday darling. And it's a wonder I'm able to write today.

The "Sirocco" has struck us! This is a wind that comes each year. Like the "Mistral" or the "Tornado" of America or the Typhoon of the South Seas.

I've never experienced anything like it.

The wind arose at 11a.m. yesterday and all work ceased. It just blew and blew at about 90-100m.p.h. Tents flew away like leaves, and huts and corrugated iron sheds flew about like a pack of cards.

And with it came the dust. So black that it blotted out the sun for hours. And this dust stings the body like red hot needles. Our eyes are sore, and red, and throats full of it. It gets into every nook and cranny and into any kit altho' it's wrapped and covered up.

All our clothes and blankets are full of dust, and we all look like miners.

The tables in the cookhouse are covered with a one eighth inch coat of dust – also the food.

It was just impossible to write, read, or do anything except just sit it out. It lasted until 8p.m. and it came again Today. From 1.30p.m. until 7.00p.m. And they tell us it goes on for 3 weeks!

Well, damn Italy! Or Foggia Plain at any rate. You should see my towel after 3 days use! It's just like the hearthrug.

Funnily enough the only building that didn't get a "doing" is the Salvation Army Hut!

Our tent stood it pretty well, as it was rigged by a Balloon Operator, and I got some rope and put on double guys all round.

Dick Waddington walked into here tonight. He is posted to Bari and en route was staying the night in Foggia.

He has just the same worry as me. He can't see how he's going to get more than £4 per week outside!

He hadn't got any special news. He's group 16 by the way. Due in Milan on Sept 1st.

I still cannot make up my mind about this post war business darling. And yet I seem to be alone in my pessimism. All the blokes seem to think it's going to be easy to get good jobs.

Well darling, there isn't very much to write about. There wasn't a letter from you today but I'm hoping for one tomorrow darling, so that there'll be something to write about.

Percy persists on talking to me (very rudely) and I just cannot concentrate on this. He just goes on and on, altho' I don't answer him

All my love darling. Please write a lot.

Always Yours

All my love

Ken xxx

L.L.&M. xxx

Sorrento   Friday 12th August 45

My Very Own Darling

At last my dear one I can embrace you, and we can rejoice together, and thank God that the <u>War</u> <u>is</u> <u>over</u>!! It is too good to be true isn't it darling. But it is true, and soon we can be together again. It is an amazing thing to think that, could we have had a dozen of these Atomic bombs in 1939, the War would not have lasted a month.

Again we must thank God that the two Germans who helped to design the bomb were pro British and not German. Do you realise that two of those bombs properly placed would have wiped out Coventry, and 4 would have seen Birmingham off the map. One of the Jerry professors was from B'ham University.

Well darling, I think we all knew a few days ago that a week would see it thru. And we were right. I am glad for all our sakes, and even the Jap children are blameless.

It is difficult to explain my feelings when I knew. My heart just felt full, and of course I thought of you and the folks at home, and I wanted to cry. I do now. It is so wonderful darling to think that I am coming home to you, just as I left you loving you as much as ever.

The news was given to Percy and me by a Yank Captain who picked us up in a jeep! He also picked up 3 merchant seamen, and the party in the jeep comprised an Englishman, a Welshman, an Irish, a Scot, a Frenchman and a Yank!!!

We careered madly alongside singing the stars and stripes, Britannia, Madelone and the Irish, English and Scotch songs. I think I was in greater danger than ever before.

All for now dear one, pushed for light, and Been up 20 hours.

Goodnight my Love your Very Own

LL&M xxx   Ken xxxx

4

So Close, Yet So Far

Foggia   Tuesday 14th Aug 45

My Own Darling

Well dear I feel a little bit better today. It is hard to know where to
begin, as it is so long since I wrote you a real letter.

I am, for me, in a unique position. I am in hospital! Being looked
after like a baby!

There is <u>nothing</u> for you to worry about darling. Following the
fever, I now have yellow jaundice (hepatitis) and some other things.
They are none of them too serious, but just prove that I am run down
with heat, bad food, bad water, lack of baths, etc.

The hospital in Foggia 1945 where Ken was incarcerated for
many weeks, delaying his demob from the RAF

And the treatment is <u>absolute</u> rest, and a very special diet. I hadn't
been in here half an hour before I was given a plate of chicken and
some nice peaches and cream. I hadn't had a meal for 4 days, and was
literally starving. My stomach has been so fussy that I could not even

97

face anything, and I only ate the chicken with difficulty and under protest.

Well dear, I can see I am going to be looked after very well, and believe me, I can do with a rest after the hours we have worked.

According to the gen here, this complaint keeps one in anything from 3 to 6 weeks <u>according to the patient</u>.

Well, this patient has something to look forward to darling. Do you realise that my work in the R.A.F. is over!?

I am supposed to be demobbed by Sept 30th so you see as soon as I get out of here I'll be on my way home darling.

Now dear there isn't anything to worry about. This is a lovely hospital in Foggia: (Taken over by the R.A.F.) and they are good to us.

I think I told you that I had received another two 200 Players on Saturday (400). It looks as if I shan't lose on the deal at all dear, as I think they will all get here in time. I also received your parcel darling but was <u>too</u> <u>ill</u> <u>to</u> <u>open</u> <u>it</u>!!

I have now done so, and am very pleased with it, but of course I can see now, that I shan't be away long enough to use the contents.

I bought some more presents at Sorrento, and I also sent you some nuts assorted. I should wash them if I were you darling.

Keep writing to the same address darling, as Percy will be bringing my letters in for me.

You will have realised that I have decided to come home to you dear.

All my love dear, this is all I can manage now for cramp etc.

Your Own

Ken xxx

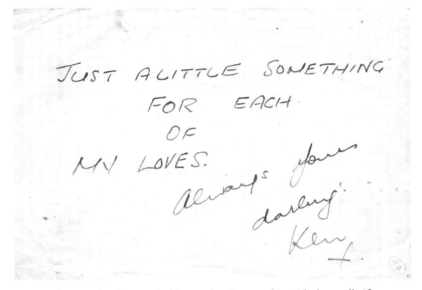

JUST A LITTLE SOMETHING
FOR EACH
OF
MY LOVES.
always your
darling.
Ken

The note that Ken put in his parcel to Ivy, together with the small gifts
he had bought for 'each of his loves' in Sorrento

Ivy and Ken must have been devastated by Ken's incarceration in a Foggia hospital due to contracting hepatitis. How ironic that this had happened just as peace had been declared and demobilisation had begun. Ken thought there was nothing to worry over, believing that he would recover rapidly. This, however, was not the case and he spent many long weeks and months in hospital.

He was confused in this letter dated 14 August and apologised for the time that had passed since he last wrote. It was, in fact, only two days.

In a subsequent letter, however, he apologised once again for not having written 'for a day or two darling'. On that occasion seven weeks had elapsed between letters.

Wednesday 15th August 1945

Ward.M.5
No 4 General Hospital

My Own Darling

I think you may as well send your letters here dear, as it looks as if I shall be here 3 weeks, and possibly 5. This is a bad show darling as I'm afraid it is going to delay my demobbing a bit. Oh well it's just one of those things and I suppose I've just got to put up with it darling.

It seems that I have had Sandfly Fever and it has left me with Yellow Jaundice. I don't feel very well dear. I am on a special diet but I can't eat anything at all, and I always feel hungry. The Sisters are very nice to us and try to make us comfortable.

The routine is just normal hospital style, which you know much better than I do.

Some of the things are a bit strange, and take a bit of getting used to – Salts! Horrible. Blood Tests. And nurses playing around regardless. But in the main it is nice to have a rest with no worry of work, and to be away from the dust and filth.

They give us plenty of cigs and sweets, but I ain't smoking now. Only about 8 in 4 or 5 days.

At last the war is really over darling. But it can't get me home any quicker now.

There's lots I want to write about darling but I go dizzy and can't think when it comes to. Please write quickly and a lot. And tell Mom and Kath that I shan't be writing. It is just too great an effort, and makes me a bit funny.

So all my love my darling.

Always your own.

Ken xxx

Ken must have felt really ill and depressed about his illness and the prolongation of his separation from Ivy. It was out of character for him to be so passive about the situation in which he now found himself. He seemed muddled about what his illness really was – sandfly fever, yellow jaundice, hepatitis – and bemused by the tests and the treatment.

22.M.F.H.   6th Oct 45

My Own Darling,

I haven't written for a day or two darling, because I thought I might
have some good news for you. I am up at last dear! I have been getting
up for 3 days now, and I shall soon be OK.

I walked about 300 yards yesterday, and believe me, it was just as
much as I could manage. I am very weak on my legs yet.

I don't quite know how long I shall be in here now, but I will try
and write and let you know tomorrow. I think it will be at least 7
days at all events. In any case, I shan't come out until I am OK because
I shall be having to hump kit about. This place isn't so good since 22
M.F.H. took over. It is only like a glorified sick quarters now, and the
food is nothing to rave about. Perhaps this is just as well tho, as it
will break me in again ready for the stuff outside.

I am glad you got your perfume, because I don't know where I
could have got any.

Well darling, it really won't be long now will it. I am eagerly looking forward to getting home now. I rather imagine that I shall be
approximately 21 days from today darling, but of course, I cannot
say definitely.

I should put the address on the back of all your letters now, as the
time is coming when I'm likely to "be gone". Then they will be
returned to you.

I haven't been out today because it has been raining like the devil.
Incidentally it has gone very cold here, and everyone is wearing heavy
duty dress now.

But it's quite cold in the hospital and the warmest place is in
bed.

Well darling I think this is just about all there is to write about so look after yourself darling, and don't forget that I love you tons and tons.

Always your Very Own

Ken x

LL&M xxx

My Darling,

I shall be on the way tomorrow. I am all fixed up now and ready to go.

As I have previously said, I expect to be mucked about a bit at Milan, so I should estimate a bit more than the eleven days, I think.

I have acquired one or two things to make the journey a bit more comfortable, such as a tin of cheese, candles, etc. (There are no lights in the Italian trains and very few windows.)

Milano, October 1945 – Ken passed through Milan
on his way home from the War

I am getting very excited now darling, and was talking my head off in my sleep last night about it. It seems as if Sunday will never come.

Don't forget to give me a chance to make a fuss of the nibs when I get home, as they don't understand so well as you do.

Well darling look after yourself, and get the fatted calf ready.
I shan't be able to write again until I get to Milan. (About Tuesday).

All my love

Darling

Your Own

Ken x

LL&M xxx

5

On the Road, 1950–1957

The war letters cease in November 1945 when Ken's duty with the RAF was drawing to a close. His last official day of service with the RAF was 11 January 1946.

Documentary evidence in the form of a reference shows that from January 1946 to February 1948, Wolf Electrical Tools in Villa Cross employed Ken as a foreman.

Perhaps he did, at some stage, also work with his brother-in-law, Fred, in the painting and decorating business. What we do know is that his fierce ambition to work with Arthur Bourne on the *Motorcycle* magazine came to nothing and this must have been a huge disappointment to him.

By 1950, it appears that Ken found work connected with the engineering trade. It meant, once again, that he would be separated from Ivy and his children. Neither of them relished this idea, but there was obviously a desperate need to earn money to support his growing family.

Darling

It isn't much use telling you that I'm fed up. But I am.

There are just two people in the Douglas. Mrs Armstrong, the owner – and me.

This room is like one out of a museum, and there is a great silence which you could cut with a knife.

The weather is a scorcher – about 75-80 degrees I should think. I worked all today and yesterday, and last night went for a stroll. Got fed up and was bathed and bedded by 9p.m. There isn't a film on worth seeing, and anyway it's too hot for that.

Mrs Armstrong is interested in Mom's two-piece – at £10. So if it isn't gone, I'll bring it up next time I come.

I found out that the nibs can have a season ticket on the bus. You have to get it from the Council House apparently.

I hope they are keeping the bit of garden tidy which I've done. And not getting rubbish on the lawn. If they are, get after 'em.

This would be just the weather for a cruise down the Clyde, but I shouldn't enjoy it without you.

Well darling, I'm just going to have my tea, and then I suppose the usual stroll, and finish up in bed with a book.

Coming home Tues.a.m.

All my love always darling

Your Own

Ken xxx

When the letters began again in 1950, Ken was once more living in 'digs' away from home and was both lonely and unhappy.

'Mom's two-piece – at £10' mentioned in this letter is surprising: £10 would have been almost a week's wages and seems expensive for a second-hand dress and jacket or a suit. Rosy died in March 1949 so perhaps Ivy and Ken were beginning to sell off some of her things to realise a bit of cash.

The season ticket for the nibs must have been a bus ticket to travel to and from school each day – obtainable from Birmingham City Council House.

Ken became absolutely furious if the girls got stones on the lawn because they would spoil the blades of the mower. As Linda was ten, Muriel eight, Lorna six and Jennifer one at the time, Ivy must have had a task on her hands to police them full-time whilst they played in the garden.

The children did have their own 'rough' lawn at the end of the garden to play on, so it was not as strict a rule as first appears.

109

Darling,

Well dear, I have found time to write this week. I was at Peacocks yesterday, and today I went over to Taylor Bros. Geographically, this place is hopeless for Taylors. It took me 1Hr 20 mins to get there this morn, and 55 mins to get back. So I'll have to look a bit further for a place near Taylors.

If they haven't already been, the firm will be calling for those sealing pliers. They rang up about 'em, and also asked me to try and postpone Peacocks to go to Rotherham, but it couldn't be did.

We get a good breakfast here, and a very reasonable evening meal. I stopped at Taylors till 7p.m. tonight to finish the job. I got plenty of help again.

I hope you can kid someone to come in on Friday night, as I am getting a bit fed up of not being able to take you out. See what you can arrange darling.

We shall have to think seriously about this business. I know that you are unhappy – just because of that. And I am miserable because I know how you feel. I love you so much darling, that you don't realize how I look forward to missing my sleep at weekends just to consciously hold you in my arms.

But if you would have it otherwise darling, then I shall have to find another job – at home.

That's going to be very difficult. I don't get any younger, and you know, I've <u>no real qualifications</u>. I only got this job on bluff! And as far as I can see it's very permanent.

I am happy in the job itself – and capable. But I am <u>not</u> happy away from you.

Then of course there's the financial angle. I suppose it's worth £10 a week really. – And it will improve.

So it's up to you darling. You must think it over and make a decision.

But of all things, I don't want to lose you. And lately, we seem to get further and further apart somehow.

Remember darling that for many years now, I have just lived for you. Sometimes you may wonder, I know, but always, you can be assured of one thing above all, and that is that I am, have been, and always will be,

Your <u>very</u> <u>own</u>

Loving

Ken xxx

Keep your pecker up darling till Friday

Yours K.

It is clear from this letter that Ken was still absent from home – he had to earn money in whatever way he could. Peacocks and Taylor Brothers were both small engineering firms in the north of England with which he was involved.

It would appear that Ivy had become heartily sick of his travelling and it was causing a serious rift in their marriage. Ken tried to address the problem by suggesting a Friday night outing (probably to the Odeon cinema or dancing at Laura Dixon's). Of course, it would not have been easy to arrange a baby-sitter for four young children – nor to obtain the extra cash needed to pay one.

Ken was desperate to resolve matters, but was in a cleft stick. He offered to try to find work at home whilst underlining the difficulties. It is quite upsetting that he felt, at the age of 48, he was too old to be able to find alternative work.

Something must have changed, however, because Ivy and Ken did start going dancing regularly. Ivy's daughters remember her excitement when she dressed up on a Friday night in a beautiful, swirling taffeta skirt ready to trip the light fantastic at Laura Dixon's. Ken bought a pair of very shiny black patent leather shoes kept especially for dancing. He was a good dancer and loved the tango and the quickstep.

They must have worked their way through this sticky patch because Ken continued to work away from home for several more years.

Another fragment

... make razor blades, and laughed it off. Two nights later the Raff came with 1200 Lancasters and Halifaxes. They dropped oil fire bombs, then phosphorous, then High Explosives, and completely wiped out Kassel. It burned for 3 days. Over 7000 known victims!! It is just fantastically unbelievable unless you see it. For once I wish I had a camera altho' I think it might not be wise to be seen taking morbid snaps.

You would think they would hate our guts, but no! We are welcomed. Their attitude is that war is war, and play is play, and when it's done, shake hands and drink together. They even say the R.A.F. is good. They fight fair. They have nothing but praise for our P.O.W. treatment. But you should hear what they've got to say about the Russians. They hate them alright.

When asked about Belsen they are obviously nauseated themselves. They explain this by saying that in any nation of many million people there will be two or three thousand murderers, sadistic cutthroats etc., who will do anything for payment. And their payment was high.

Well, so much for the war. After that their first aim was to get trade going as quickly as possible, and to this end they have cleared about 20 or 30 feet each side of the main streets and built up quickly prefabricated shops. Any big building which still had any girders standing was quickly filled up with breeze blocks and got going again. They have used wallboard – paper and cardboard, and even compressed straw for ceilings and dividing walls. Won't last long, and I'm sure some of it isn't safe. However trade is going on. And what shops! A beaten race! Ha. Ha. They are right out in front of Switzerland. Can't make it out. Everything in the shops is good and cheap. They are short of nothing. There are no poor. And everyone is well dressed. Could spend all the firm's money in an hour!

There is so much I would like to buy for us all. There is so much variety that you just <u>don't</u> know which to choose. For instance briefcases and handbags. In one shop window alone there will be perhaps <u>80 </u>briefcases and <u>50</u> or <u>60</u> handbags. Out of these 80 there will be 30 @ £2 to £3, 30 @ £3 to £4, and the rest you'd give your soul for.

Same applies to Travel Bags, Suit Cases, Shoes, handbags. Gents and ladies dressing sets, purses, wallets, etc. etc. Their long suit is leather, it is just fantastic.

I might tell you I regret I didn't have more cash with me. But if I come back, watch out. I have already been offered £8 for my coat. (Their suits and coats are probably their poorest quality line.)

I know it sounds ridiculous but here is a list of things I've seen which really interest me so far. I would like your opinion.

The list is missing!

Another idea I have is to possibly try sending a fairly cheap parcel home and see what happens.

After seeing the linen here, I just cannot make out why she bothered with Mom's stuff. Every present she gave us was of the cheapest. The hairbrushes are 5/- each. The clock was about 17/6d.!! Just junk.

Anyway let me know immediately your ideas, and make a definite priority list, because I don't want to do the wrong thing. I shall not make any purchase until I hear from you.

Also if there is any thing that you want that I haven't mentioned, let me know, as it's probably cheap. Eau de Cologne 4711 is about 35/- per quarter pint. All perfumes are very dear. But if you <u>do</u> want any, tell me which sort.

Tell Fred I am 200 miles from Frankfurt. Haven't seen a book for him yet. But I am going to make enquiries.

Well darling this is about all for now. Shall post this on Friday 14th ins. At 9.a.m.

Look after yourself darling and think of me. All my love to you and the children.

Your very own

Ken xxx

P.S. Envelopes in Bureau but make them <u>plain</u>! I am not bothered about newspapers. Send Autocar. Magazine wrappers in right hand pigeon hole of bureau. Love. K.

Look after yourself darling, and keep your pecker up. Let me know if there are any special items that you want, bearing in mind that I won't want to attract too much attention at the customs this time.

Lots of love, always your own, Ken xxxx

Ken fitting a train bearing in Germany in 1951
when he was working for British Timken

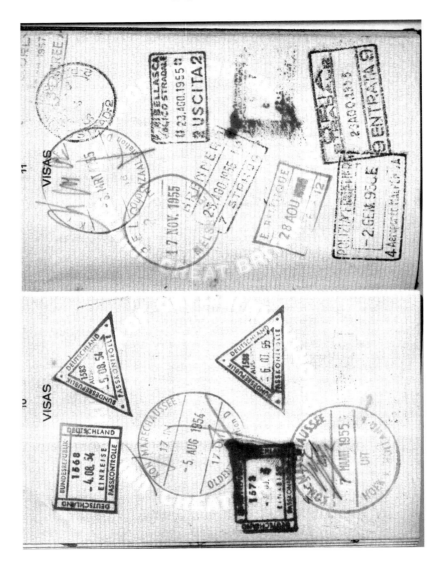

Ken's well-stamped passport occasionally caused problems at the Customs.

This fragmented letter mentions Kassel, which would mean that Ken had started working for British Timken. He spent several years in Germany, Switzerland and Italy helping to restore railway systems that had been decimated by war.

Although part of the letter is missing, we can guess that Ken was writing home about the effect of war on Germany and the peculiar situation he found himself in – working for a people that his earlier duty had been to fight.

It is a shame that the list is missing. Ken did bring home some lovely leather goods. His girls had beautiful leather dressing cases containing glass bottles, toothbrush holders, soap dishes, clothes and hairbrushes, mirrors and manicure items. Ivy had a wonderful mosaic jewellery box that played music whilst a delicate ballerina danced, her movements reflected tenfold in the mirrored lid. Ken had a very smart briefcase, as did daughter Muriel, as she was due to move to King Edward's Grammar School.

When Ken's mother died his sister, Kath, ransacked the family home, taking all the linen and silverware away. This rankled with Ken and he writes of his puzzlement at her miserly behaviour. Kath was stationed in Germany with the American Red Cross throughout the war and for many years afterwards and could easily have obtained quality items. She could, of course, have wanted her mother's possessions for purely sentimental reasons.

Ken's offer to bring things home was probably risky. Because he went back and forth so regularly between Britain and Europe, his passport was stamped over and over again. The customs officers did become suspicious and he was often searched. Years later when he took his family abroad he was still using the same well-stamped passport and on one occasion the car was practically ripped apart.

Dear Children,

Just a line to let you know that I am getting along well in Kassel. I miss you all a lot, and especially the racket you make after you're supposed to be asleep at night.

As your mother has told you, this town was bombed dreadfully by the R.A.F. in the war, and is almost flattened to the ground. But the ordinary Germans like your mommy and I, do not hate us for this. They think that it was their duty to fight us and to put up with the bombing. They were only being loyal to their Dictator or Leader, who was a man like our Kings and Queens.

But now it is over, they are very friendly, and glad for us to come and spend our money here, and to trade with them. In fact tonight I was talking to a German who was in the Luftwaffe, (The German Air Force). He was a bomb aimer, and he got shot down by a Spitfire, and was badly wounded. But we had a good joke together, and laughed to think we were in opposite air forces in the war.

This area around here, Hessenland, was the home of the Kaisers, the old 'Kings' of Germany. There are beautiful parks, and a wonderful Schloss, (or castle) where the Kaisers used to live in the summer. This place is called the WILHELMSHOHE PALACE (pronounced WILLEMSHOOER). It is a very beautiful 'castle' and as it is a little out in the country, was not too badly bombed.

But although the Germans suffered so much in the war, they are not down hearted. They work night and day to re-build the towns. And by working hard and for many hours it means there is plenty of lovely food in the shops. There is no rationing, and they have many lovely foods and things that English children have never seen.

They are determined to enjoy their Xmas, and go in for it in a bigger way than we do. Although the town council has little money to spare, they have decorated the place for Xmas. All down what is left of the main streets they have put up white painted pine poles about 35 feet high and every 25 yards. These are gaily decorated with fir branches, fairy lights and silver trimmings. The shops in the main street, (which of course are only like shop windows with no proper shop above, or at the back), and which have been quickly built over the ruins, are beautifully decorated in a way that I have never seen at home. Xmas trees with beautiful trimmings. Father Christmases driving sleighs pulled by Reindeer on clouds of cotton wool floating in the windows.

Angels and cherubs flying in sky scenes. Father Christmases in the shops, and the children having their photographs taken with him. All the toys and presents in the shops layed out with pretty labels and holly. And they seem to change the windows every two or three days. After the shops are closed at night they put curtains over the windows, and work until the early hours to make a new window dressing for the people to see next day.

If one buys anything in a shop; presents, butter, sugar – anything it is wrapped in pretty Christmas paper and stuck up with lovely labels.

I wish you could be here to see it, as I am afraid you'll never see anything so wonderful in England.

And the countryside is all covered with snow. The fir forests look very pretty, just as you see them in the Xmas cards and pictures. The snow does not seem to be like our snow. This is clean and dry. And not messy like it is at home. The temperature is always below zero and it is very cold. All the children wear special clothes to keep out the cold. And by the way they are at school at 8 0'clock in the morning, and they all learn English as a normal subject.

I have met Father Christmas and he says that if you are very good, and help your mommy, he might even fly all the way from Germany on Christmas night. But you'll have to be very good.

The children here have been sledging and skiing now for a fortnight, and they really do enjoy it.

And I know from what I see now, that they will all have a Very Merry Xmas.

This is all for now and soon I'll be home again.

With all my love,

Daddy xxxx

Hotel Auriga, Milano   Friday 1955

My Darling

Well, I reached a stage where there was nothing else left to write about; and now all of a sudden; there is.

I had a pot of tea and drank 4 cups, and after a while, reached a stage where I was bursting "to go upstairs". So I entered the lift, and got somewhere between the 3rd and 4th floors when all the power in Milan went off! I was stuck in a small cubicle in pitch darkness.

I could hear sounds of panic, but no-one took any notice of me. After about 5 minutes it dawned on me that they did not know I was there! So I started tapping out ---. . .---. . . S.O.S.

Then the panic really started. Meester B----- where are you? We are very sorry, what can we do? So I said "Bore a hole in the floor so that I can do a pee." They took it seriously and said if it is urgent "You must do it, do not worry." Anyway after much tussling they got the lift down somehow by hand close to the 2nd floor. They managed to open it up, and my head was level with their feet. I got hauled out. The Manager was nearly having a stroke about a guest being treated so badly and called for a stiff Brandy.

I told him I reckoned it was me ought to have a drink – not him, so he called for a Martini for me. Then two Americans came in, and one said, "No Sir, I'm Hirem K Biglow from N'York, no sir, I don't climb 5 flights for no man, I guess I better find another Hotel!"

So – Drinks for them – and candles. Finished up, free drinks for everyone in the damn place. People milling round, no-one would climb the stairs. General Panic. Finally power came back after 2 hours or so. I think half of Italy was affected.

And sunny Italy! <u>Minus</u> 18 degrees <u>centigrade</u>!!! That is 14 degrees F. or 18 degrees of Frost. The Itis are all crying with the cold. They completely turban their heads with scarves, just leaving a peep hole

121

to look out of. The men are wearing their wives' fur around their necks, and cloaks, and ponchos, and wot have you.

There is at least a foot of hard frozen snow all over Italy.

And wot about the weather at home, you did not tell me, but how about the enclosed cutting? Hope you've got enough coal. And I don't know how you're getting on for firewood? You'd better get a few firelighters or something. I don't want you to chop your fingers off. Anyway most of the wood is damp.

At least 24 axles have arrived at Breda. At the same time got called to Pistoia (where I am) only to find it a fools errand!

Arrived here Thursday late and am going to stay tonight (nice bath here) and go back to Milan on Saturday.

Train delayed in mountains by snow ploughs. Ice <u>inside</u> windows never thawed out in a seven hour journey. Very cold trip. Wind howled here last night like nothing I've ever heard before, but I took all the blankets off the twin bed and had a very good night after all.

 The sun is now shining beautifully, but it's impossible to stand in the wind for more than a minute or two.

Hope you haven't had any <u>drifting</u> fine snow, in the roof. If you suspect it, you <u>must</u> get Fred or Frank to do something about it. But <u>don't</u> you get up and certainly <u>not</u> any of the children. It's a dangerous business.

Well darling, I'm afraid you won't get this until Monday, altho' it is just possible with luck, that it could catch a plane direct from Florence, in which case you could be lucky for Saturday.

I don't know whether I told you but I made a great effort and wrote to Kath! How does Lorna think she got on?

Have written to M.O.T and Civil Service for a job as a road vehicle examiner at £850. For once they <u>don't</u> want <u>young</u> <u>men</u>! Minimum age 35. Accepted up to 50. Extra marks for War Service. Could be just the job.

All my love darling. More on Sunday.

Your very own Ken xxxx

The frequent underlining in the paragraph about the snow probably got Ivy's back up. After all, she had endured years and years of managing all sorts of situations on her own. The children at this time were still young and it was highly unlikely that Ivy would have considered sending them up into the loft to clear snow. She probably would not have needed Ken to point this out!

It is interesting to note that Ken was softening towards his estranged sister, Kath. From other documents that have come to light, it seems Ivy wished to encourage their correspondence and it did grow significantly as the years went by. Sadly, they were not to meet face to face again. Kath died alone in San Francisco in 1984.

'How does Lorna think she got on?' is probably a reference to her having recently sat the entrance examination for a place at grammar school. (She passed.)

The final paragraph demonstrates that Ken was still trying to find work that did not involve travelling away from home. MOT was the Ministry of Transport: 'For once they don't want young men!'

Ken was all of 42. Today we would consider 42 as being young!

Hotel Auriga, Milan   18th Tuesday 1954

Darling,

Just a hurried note. I wish you were here to see this fabulous town of
Florence – Wonderful. But seeing it in a hurry in the rain, in the
dark!

    Got up at 5.30am early train to Florence and Pistoia – 300 miles.
Got here at 1.30. Lunch. Then at the works all afternoon until 6pm.
One hour back to Florence. Found a hotel, found a meal and then
had a high speed walk round. Dead beat. Gone mad. Going by luxury
coach tomorrow at 8.00am to Pisa, La Spezia and Genoa. But it will
take till 6pm to cover 250 miles. Then train 60 miles to Milan. Barmy
but I think it will be worth it.

    Learning how to eat. Watched a young chicken roasted on a spit
over a charcoal fire here, and then ate it, Italian fashion, with my
fingers. Wonderful.

All my love darling,

Your very own

Ken xxx

? Hows Dad going on?

'Dad' mentioned in the postscript to this letter was Ivy's father.
He was ill at the time of writing and died soon after.

Hotel Auriga, Milan

Darling,

Just made a mad dash to catch the coach for Genoa. No-one could tell me where it started. When zero hour arrived I really began to get the wind up. However finally found a coach driver who directed me properly. Just arrived in time and we were off.

These long distance luxury coaches are run like an airline with a Hostess. Like a conducted tour. Detours are made to places of interest on the way. We were first slowly driven around Montecatini, a noted salt spring health resort. Next call Pisa. Guide laid on. Conducted over Cathedral and Leaning Tower. Then a diversion to the house of the late Puccini. (Some American dame asked loudly all over the 'bus, "who was this guy Puccini"??!!)

Now we are stopped at Viareggio, a famous Italian seaside resort, for lunch.

This is a swindle. They have kidded most of the people to take the set lunch which will cost them a bundle. I am settling for a quarter of roast chicken again with rolls and beautiful butter. Some vino Chianti and then a coffee. (Oh for a cup of proper tea.) Have forgotten what it tastes like now.

The weather is now glorious again, just like our later summer, and I am too hot in just 3 things. Have to wear sun specs most of the time. I think this coach stunt is really the best way to travel here, and I shall probably do some more of it later.

The lunch has now arrived at the table so more later on darling. This seems awful waste, being alone darling. Hope I shan't be long now. Dammit no more paper!

Just begged another piece of paper from the Restaurant so can continue.

Have finished the chicken. Just don't know how they cook it but it's marvellous. I think it is always basted over an open fire like the Ancient Britons used to eat 'em.

Am now having a strong black coffee, and very shortly we carry on our way.

The next part of the "tour" is a corker! About 80 miles of Stelvio like roads, overlooking the sea on one side.

I was advised against making this trip, because it is supposed to be very sick-making.

The coach is complete with toilet and Refreshments! Primitive Italians what?

Lord only knows what time I shall get to Milan. We aren't due in Genoa until 7.00pm and then it's another 60 miles or so.

I hope there may be a letter waiting when I get there. I am looking forward to it a lot darling.

Going to try and post this now. So all my love for a while.

Your Very Own

Ken xxx

Hotel Auriga Milano

Darling,

There doesn't seem to be very much to write about. I have finished at Milan and there will be no more work there until the next order commences in September or October.

I am going to Pistoia tomorrow to see what is doing there. I have already tried to book a return flight, and much to my surprise all flights are fully booked at B.E.A. already!

I managed to get a flight on Air Italia for the 30th. So I shall be back somewhere about 9.30 to 10p.m.

Can't make the weather out here. It is beautifully sunny and warm but there's a very keen wind all the time which cuts the hands without gloves. But further south in Rome area 400 villages are cut off with snow! They say this weather is absolutely un-precedented this year.

I walked back from the works one afternoon. It took me 2 hours and I got a whopping blister under my foot. Today I walked around Milan for 3 hours, and got another one! Don't know whether it is the socks or the unusual exercise!? I don't think it's the socks!

If you write it had better be to Hotel Milano, Pistoia, Near Florence. But don't send anything later than the 27th because it might not get there.

All for now

Lots of Love,

Ken xxx

Hotel Erzherzog Rainer
Wien, Austria

Darling,

Well here we are in Vienna. This is a city of wonderful buildings, boulevards etc. and is truly beautiful. We haven't been in any buildings yet except the Cathedral, which is normal. We'll get around to that later.

This is a pretty expensive hotel, and it is almost a la Savoy, the service is wonderful. Tho' the bath trouble is the same. There just ain't any showers or private baths in Austria. Here it works very fast. The chamber maids sit out on the landing waiting for the bell to ring. But it costs _five_ English shillings!! (Henceforth I shall quote prices in English.) So we ain't having many baths. We are making do with a rub down in our rooms.

We have a separate room each with an inter connecting door, so altho' we are together we can be apart. In fact when we are bathing etc. we do respect each other's privacy.

We are ringing for the usual sundry pots of tea in our room, tho' Lord knows what they'll cost. In fact we have just had breakfast in our room at 10.30a.m. (Damn nuisance but a blasted brass band and religious procession woke us up early.)

On this cold morning we are sitting writing in pants only. The temperature is 80.6 degrees!!! If we go out in the midday sun it is over 100!!!

The clothing issue has been forced. We have just <u>had</u> to go and order sub tropical suits. Even if I have to pay myself, it had to be done. I have ordered one fairly good one (at £12.10.0.) in light sort of fawn. Johnny has had one cheaper one for work for now at £9. Later, when permission comes, he will probably get some better ones.

Of course, either way, I shan't pay, as you know, but I think we shall get the O.K. We also have bought 2 short sleeved Terylene shirts, which also we shall book.

The heat is just terrific. One can sit in an outside restaurant at 11 p.m. in perfect comfort in just slacks and shirt. But altho' holiday makers and ordinary people go about like this, and also wear shorts, business people keep jackets on. – But not our kind.

We have gone mad. Johnny wanted a portable radio and I told him that of course, he could buy one right away. But I suggested a good idea would be to get a second hand one (because of customs later). So we looked around but could find nothing. But one of the evenings we decided to take a "short Cut" to our pet café and lo and behold the first corner we turned, there was a Radio shop with 2 second hand portables at about £5.10.0. each. (The new price is £15.) The shop was closed but J. said he liked the red one. I myself was very tempted because as you know I have always wanted one for abroad, and travelling.

So next day we went in, and they were beautiful little sets. (About as big as our Mystery of Life book.)

They played beautifully. So we knocked him down to £4.10s. for buying the two!

I don't know what the hotel think, but we had them delivered marked "Radios. Fragile". An hour later a bod turned up with 4 shirts, and on Monday, they'll arrive with the suits.

If you want any shoes for Jen and Lorna (and possibly M.) wait until you get to Austria. Beauties for about 25/-. But ours are about the same. Otherwise as far as I can see there are no bargains except for shirts.

If there is anything in which you are particularly interested, let me know and I will spy out the land.

I would like to bring you to Vienna if it was only just to ride round and <u>look</u> at the buildings, and this could praps be an idea for our spare day.

I would also like to take the kids to the Pratesplatz, that is the Play Place, or the Vienna permanent fair.

Yesterday as we had Sat to kill we went down there after our shopping and did a Harry Lime on the big wheel. It is a wonderful fair. The miniature train does a half hour trip through the Vienna woods for 1/3d adults and 6d for kids and all the prices are 3d to 6d for children. Also there are always special kids merry go rounds etc.

You can leave 'em for an hour to ride 2 wheel bikes, trikes, or cars in special enclosure with sign posts, tunnels, traffic lights, the lot. It's really wonderful.

We came away at 10 o'clock and got lost! We just tramped and tramped. However, we finally made out.

The whole of Friday was spent seriously in doing technical drawings for the job. And of course tomorrow, we hope to do some work.

I don't know if I told you, but nothing has arrived except for 52 tender boxes. These should go on in 2-3 days, and then we are out of work. If the stuff <u>does not arrive fairly</u> quickly, I can foresee me being delayed a little. But don't worry darling. As soon as I am happy about Johnny, I will get away.

Meanwhile, I will try and make this up to you with the best holiday you've ever had.

If there is anything you want within reason for the hol, get it and it will be O.K.

But first let me know because some things may be either cheaper, or more attractive here. (Like those raffia skirts in Italy for instance.)

We are right in the first team at this hotel. The Manager downwards is giving us the best of service. Because: The other day, we had a pot of tea and a few cakes in our room. One cake was <u>mouldy</u>. (J. just happened to turn it over.) So in order not to embarrass them (like a yank) I wrote the complaint on a note, and gave it to the Head Porter as we went out.

On our return at 11p.m. there was a note from the manager in each of our pigeon holes. Would we kindly grant <u>him</u> an interview. Profuse apology. Outside bakery and God wot. "In future Sir, I assure you, our service shall be faultless." And now it is obvious <u>everyone</u>, <u>everyone</u>, has been told to grovel to us.

Well darling if you need cash. Go to the Bank. I can pay you straight back.

For now darling,

All my love, Your very own

Ken xxx

Vienna

July 1955
Wed

Darling,

Got your note at Vienna this A.M. Called at Am Spitz and picked up the other letters.

It is now 2p.m. (at the works) and I shall despatch the letter to France this p.m. together with this one to you.

Can't understand your 8 days. You could get this on Friday and I could get a reply for Monday (one day less if it wasn't for Sunday).

There is nothing to do about the R.A.C. at the moment, unless there is any development from their travel Dept re holiday. (But that is not too urgent.)

But I would like you to telephone Smithfield Garage. Digbeth (Service Manager) and ask them if in fact the Pru have given them the OK to proceed with the repairs, and how they're getting on with it. You can tell him fairly that there is no <u>desperate</u> hurry. (I don't want them to rush it.) But point out that I <u>could</u> want it in another 2 weeks. Remind them that if it is in the way, to bring it home, and not to store it outside. Ask them to supply 2 new pedal rubbers.

If they have <u>not</u> had the O.K. from the Pru, then ring the Accident Dept, and ask them what the Hell they're messing at. (I don't need to tell you how to explain the real urgency.)

I imagine from your lack of remarks that you have heard nothing more about the accident from other sources? But I think I told you to open all mail in case there is anything of importance?

As usual, we have heard Sweet Fanny Adams from B.T. Both my letter and telegram have been ignored so far!

We can only conclude that Howard is away. Anyway we've bought the suits so we'll talk about who pays for 'em later.

Today it has gone cold. (It is <u>down</u> to about 75.) But it is improving, and if the clouds move over, I imagine it will be about 90.

No, we have seen nothing of the Vienna Festival, and don't want to. It consists of concerts in all the Halls, Opera Houses and Palaces. Concerts in each one separately for Bach, Haydn, Schubert, Mozart and Lizt, etc. We could not find the Litz concert or we may have tried that one. Johnny, like us, is not very interested in old castles and churches.

We shall most likely take our weekend pleasure by going on a boat trip up the Danube. Or a days swimming and sunbathing. By the way, how are your skins! I shed all mine, feet as well, but am now nicely browned off.

But for several days I had no ankles. My feet were so swollen and bad, as to almost necessitate taxi travel. However, they are now fully recovered.

Who sings our Green Door Record? The radios are going very well now, and are indeed a great pleasure.

Yes, we are enjoying Vienna, but of course in my usual mild sort of way. I am happier here than in Milan or Florence. (But of course I have company.) But <u>all the people</u> are more friendly. The food in particular is much cheaper, but this simply means that twice 5/- is 10/-, whereas, twice 10/- is £1 !!!???

Howsomever, it won't work out so badly (I hope).

All is going smoothly at the works now, but still no arrival of other components, tho' they were expected within a week.

It takes us an hour to travel to the works by the way. It is like going from Victoria Square, out to Walsall, with 25 minutes walking on top. (This should reduce some fat.)

All for now, I think darling, and you should get this Friday.

All my love darling,

Your very own

Ken xxx

P.S. You can tell people the shorts are sold. (If not too late.) I have other ideas.   K.

The instructions to Ivy about how she was to persuade Smith-field Garage to deal with the repairs to Ken's accident-dam-aged car must have taxed her patience to the limit. It was more than a little uncommon for women to deal with such matters at that time, and Ivy must have felt quite uncomfort-able about tackling the garage and giving them such direct orders. Ken also gave her quite specific instructions on how to deal with the insurance company: '. . . ask them what the Hell they're messing at.'

The question 'Who sings on our Green Door Record?' would have been an easy one for Ivy to answer. She was absolutely mad about Frankie Vaughan and was a lifelong fan – still going to his concerts when she was in her seventies. Ken was always teasing her about her crush on the singer – but in a good-natured fashion.

The reference to 'shorts' probably meant lederhosen. Ken used to bring sets home from Germany as people fancied them for their children. He had a set himself and wore them quite often, complete with bib, braces, bells and bits of em-broidered edelweiss. Selling shorts was probably just another way of supplementing his income.

Ivy with singing star Frankie Vaughan; she was a lifelong fan

Darling,

Yesterday we decided to try the famous swimming bath. But first we had to buy trunks and a towel. I had to pay 25/- in the finish but they are very good quality and worth it. Black with a Black and White check elastic belt. Zip pocket for Cubicle Key.

A very good bath towel cost 17/6d and it is ours altho' I shall book the towel for "the works". It is a beauty in Black and White check squares.

We paid 2/9d for a cubicle for 2 for the day. Arrived at about 1p.m. and stayed until 6.30. It is a marvellous place. 3 baths, with tiers of seats for watchers. Kids Bath. Deep swimmers bath and a very deep diving bath with boards up to 30 feet high. Showers, shops, stalls, and restaurant.

You eat in between swims and sun-bathing and just sit in the trunks. Wonderful.

Everybody goes! Women just like your Mom! In shorts, or brief swim suits. Old men like Cowper and old Harvey. Old girls like Daisy and Mrs Cowper. Ugly ones, fat ones, thin ones, grey ones, bald ones, and glamour. J. says he thinks he will probably go potty.

It is awfully funny to see a woman in a bathing suit, (mostly one piece like yours) walking gently along pushing her baby in an Italian type streamlined pram.

It's sort of like a man walking down New Street in a pair of Y front trunks and gum boots.

I wish I could take you lot there for a day. And believe me darling, you don't have to worry about exposing your figure. Some of 'em are awful freaks. But they all do it, regardless.

There are life guards on duty, and they have whistles which they blow, and then point at the offender who may be larking about too much.

About 80% of 'em look like Jamaicans, but there <u>are</u> some local white people. But I suggest you all try to get a bit of tan in the garden in readiness. Because I imagine these same conditions will maintain at any of the bathing spots. It now looks as tho' we know how to spend the spare day!

Today our <u>inside</u> thermometer went up to 115 degrees and busted. (Burst) We have been afraid to go out as it must have been about 120 in the sun!

It is now 3.34p.m. and we are going to sally forth and try it. I think the shops will all be shut, but if not, I <u>must</u> now buy a panama hat. And I <u>shall</u> book it.

They have <u>still</u> not replied to any letters, so on Wednesday we wrote again to ask if it had gone stray. There is now <u>no question</u> of wearing English clothes.

Tomorrow we may go swimming or on a boat on the Danube, which is wot we are now going to make enquiries about.

More when I get back.

Eventually got out at about 4.30p.m. Had to wait whilst my new slacks were pressed. (After I've made a slight alteration to 'em.) The heat was absolutely stifling. Just like walking past a blast furnace door all the time. Temp about 118 in the sun, and 95 in the shade.

Now we are back in the "cool" of the evening at 7.30p.m. We can stand no more. In this room it is now 85 degrees, I have taken everything off except my watch, and have pinned a thin hand towel round me like a loin cloth. Every time I move my wrist, it is stuck to the desk with sweat, and my bare rear is stuck to the chair!

Said loin cloth lets in more air than pants.

We went into a beautiful park for a meal and ordered Orangeade (iced), Salad with Hard boiled eggs and bread, butter and cheese. They brought two bowls of lettuce, plate of cheese, Butter, bread and 4 boiled eggs with <u>egg cups</u> and spoons.

Before an audience of about a hundred eyes, and also the "passing show", we proceeded to peel the eggs, cut 'em up, and make ourselves a salad. Even the waitress's eyes popped a bit. However it was very enjoyable and we just sat and sat.

After a while, we raised enough energy to <u>slowly</u> stroll back. Now the effort of writing is making me sweat all over so this is all for now darling.

My Got you'd want the iced lolly here! (But it would be nice.)

All my love darling,

Your own

Ken xxxxxx

Love to the Knibs xxxx

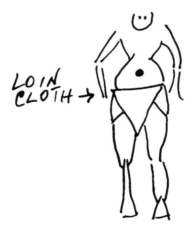

The old men and women mentioned in this letter were Ivy and Ken's neighbours in Aldridge Road. Ken appeared to be amazed by the 'types' that frequented the swimming baths.

Ken had a very tight itinerary planned for his family's first grand tour of Europe with only one spare day left for relaxing. It seems from this letter (and a couple of others) that by the time the tour was under way there would be no such thing as a spare day!

Ken did buy a panama hat and wore it for many years with great panache. He would often use old ties or bits of patterned silk or an old Paisley cravat to make a new band for the rim. Long after he finished working abroad he would wear the panama whilst pottering in the garden, or on sunny days out. Although it is now dented and battered it has been stored carefully away in a family treasure-box.

Hotel Erzherzog Rainer   12p.m.Friday 1955
Vienna   (end July)

Darling,

This is ridiculous. The weather is so severe that Vienna Radio have
just run a special programme about it. At 7.30a.m. it was 96F. At
4.30p.m. it was 127F, and now it is 90.

I don't know how we are standing it. I am sitting naked on a towel
which is getting wetter and wetter. My arms are making pools on the
desk. Have just had an ice cold rub down. Wonderful for 5 mins, but
now sweating again. Today we have drunk 4 bottles of iced lemonade,
2 pots tea, 2 glasses of iced milk each, and eaten almost nothing.

There is no question of going to bed. Last night, which was cooler
(at 85) we had no sleep at all. Tonight it seems useless to try.

We are to start serious work on Monday. Couldn't go today because
equipment not ready altho' components all here.

So today we went with Dr (Fred) Deiker in his car to Meck. Terrible journey. Dirt roads and heat absolutely unbearable (90 kilometres).
(Got help us if we get these temperatures in August.)

Came back on a Danube steamer. 5 hours (7/6d) and altho' it was
very pleasant, the boat was packed, and everybody trying to bag the
rare bits of shade. We were very glad to come ashore at the end.

At the dock, the trains were impossible. Absolutely packed like
sardines, and the heat walloping about in chunks. We just could not
face it, so treated ourselves to a big Mercedes Taxi at 5/-. Taxis are
cheap funnily enough. (4 miles.)

I am informed that we shall not get a driving cannon box until
August 1st, so I wrote to Howard and told him that I am planning
to show J. the first 4 coupled c.boxes and to try and return for W/E
13th. (Thursday I hope.) And I told him that I shall not extend my
visit unless he sends a telegram. I am going to be very annoyed if he
does, but I have told him that I want to get home darling.

I also pointed out that the next Italian visit does not give me much time for preparing for my holiday. So I have done all I can darling, and probably stuck my neck out a bit.

You may get this on Monday, and could write me again if you wish. Johnny will be able to return any letters this time. This would be nice if I did get held up. If H. should telegraph; then I will telegraph you.

Now we have Sat and Sun to waste more's the pity. In this heat public transport is out, and I also think it is too hot for stripping off to swim. It's too hot to lie on the bed, and too cold to lie on a block of ice. So I don't know what we'll do.

We have found out where they get the hidden bits brown. On top of the changing rooms there are glass (frosted) surrounded sun traps, and they prance about up there in the rude. Men and women separate buildings. But we have not got the nerve for this.

Also we are told there is an area by the Danube where everyone goes around with nowt on. Not a club. Not fenced off. Just on the side of the river.

But also told that it is mainly frequented by about 5000 dirty old men, and horrible fat old women! Supposed to be very repulsive. Again, we ain't interested. (Am now stuck to towel.)

I think J. is affected even more than I am by the heat. I don't know how he'll stick it when he hasn't got my moral support.

It was a wonderful thrill to get two letters this morning. This means a lot to me. Glad to hear the car is finished. It's funny we've heard no more from anyone about the accident.

So you see those free films are definitely a waste of time. I won't use any more of them. Linda's were on French film!

Hope Linda pulls it off O.K. but not to worry.

So you've started reading Autocars. Save 'em for me dear. (But don't forget Jaguar publicity does not sell Morris Minors.)

I will write the I. Tax bloke from here. I thought Linda's pay went on until she starts work. (Wot's the use of getting rises?)

If you see Percy, tell him to get his shorts "tailored" a bit. He'll be right out of fashion here without 'em. It <u>has</u> to be shorts, or semi tropic suits. If August/Sept temperatures are as expected, ordinary slacks will kill him.

Another thing, we'll have to put the loose covers in the car again to stop the leather burning us. The rear seat ones (in the shed) can be washed. And I think the front seat "backs" are O.K. T'others will probably have to be renewed.

Fred is finding us a nice clean Gasthof for the night of Sept 3rd in Salzburg. He says we <u>must</u> go there. He also says it is a crime to come to Austria without going over the Grossglockner.

He checked my proposed route, and volunteered the fact that he could not understand how I could know so much about Austria, and yet miss this out. He is going to be very upset if we don't go. And he wants to meet the party in Salzburg.

The insurance bloke is quite potty. The renewal notice which you sent is actually a cover note for 15 days! Until the 18th July. He's only worried about his commission. Tell him to leave his address and I'll send a cheque when I get home. Because of the accident, I think I <u>must</u> renew with the Pru.

Even our pens must be in love. You will notice that mine also has run dry. (Refills for both are in Milan.)

Well darling I think this really is about all for now, but I won't close it in case there is any other information in Sat mornings post.

By the way I now think we have "made" the holiday.

Only none of those blighters have replied about exes.

But Fred Deiker has pretty well put us right.

I wish you were here darling to thrill me, hot as it is. But this temperature seems to have killed Kelly off!! J. says he can't understand "Fagin" either for he also seems to be suffering.

All my love darling,

Your own,

Ken xxxxx

This effort has really made me sweat (1.a.m.)

The family's first European Grand Tour in 1955.
Ken used the timer on his camera so that he could be in the shot

'Hope Linda pulls it off OK but not to worry' probably refers to either school-leaving examinations or her application for a formal apprenticeship with Raymond at his Hairdressing Salon in Birmingham. Linda would have been nearly sixteen when this letter was written.

Ken was obviously concerned about money again. He threatens to write to the Income Tax assessor and wonders why the family allowance for Linda was coming to an end before she had even started work. His frustration was obvious . . . 'Wot's the use of getting rises?'

Ken reassures Ivy that the money for the holiday is secure . . . 'By the way I now think we have "made" the holiday'.

There is a very rare mention of the physical relationship between Ivy and Ken in this letter. Ken was never an openly demonstrative man – he thought kissing was 'soppy' and called it 'gum-sucking'. He certainly never made a suggestive remark or told a risqué joke in front of his girls.

Ken was a great sewer and would have had no problem at all with altering his trousers. He was often to be seen darning his socks, sewing patches on canvas tents, making car seat covers, recovering easy chairs, stitching leather elbows on jumpers and such like.

A rare, and revealing, innuendo in the final paragraph of this letter!

Hotel Milano, Pistoia
(I hope)

Darling,

I am sitting at an outside café table on the station at Prato – and it looks as if I'm going to be here for a long time!

I was glad to get your note with the grub, because it was so unexpected.

Got to London in a filthy train, and then proceeded to Waterloo only to find that the "Grosvenor" is at Victoria! Started to dash back across just as the tubes were closing, (11.30p.m. on Sundays) and just made it.

Arrived at the Airport on Monday to travel Air Italia, and found they were on strike! Got very hopeful, and then it was decided that B.E.A. would put a Viscount on. At the last minute the strike was called off and finally went in an Iti plane which did everything bar loop the loop.

The weather upstairs was rough except over France where they have Summer. Still tons of snow in the Alps. Very surprising. Then ran into Rain, Ice, and bumps, and landed at Malpensa in pouring rain!

Met a cockney couple who were on a private "conducted tour" for two. Their itinerary gave them about one and a half hours to get a train for Rimini at Milan. The coach takes 75 minutes and there was the customs to go thro'!

I told them it could not be done, even if they knew the way and the lingo. However they wanted to try so I took 'em in hand.

(Just found out there is a train in 10 mins instead of 2 hours as stated on the board.)

On arrival at Milan I grabbed a taxi and directed him pronto. Told these folks they would arrive to see the train pull out – which they

145

did – just that! That left them stranded for 3 hours to finally arrive at Rimini at 12p.m. – or go tomorrow.

They decided to travel late, and the woman then said she didn't care so long as she could get a <u>nice cup of tea!!!</u>

I did a loud guffaw and put her wise. Finally we all walked across to the Auriga and had some of my tea and they killed time in the lounge. It was still teeming torrential rain by the way. This little manoeuvre got me a free ride in the taxi so I scored there, and also they bought me a drink. Fish and chip shop owners from Islington. Got invited to call when in London – and for the first time in my life got invited to become a Mason!

Finally they left and I settled down to await a call from Harris, which came at about 6p.m. Went round to his place to look at the biggest T.V. in Italy. Cost 300,000 lire. (£165)

He was very affable and we had coffee and liqueurs and he told me Tuckey is doing Milan/Florence and Venice for their hols.

He's putting them into hotels which will cost them 12000 lire per night for the room! But so far he has not even been able to obtain rooms at <u>any</u> price for Venice! This has caused Tuck to postpone his hols to July 26th.

Went to bed at 1a.m. and slept until 11a.m. Had Brunch and then pushed off for Pistoia. Train classes have now been altered to 1st and 2nd class only, which means that the spitting, smoking, garlic eating peasants are now climbing all over the trains.

So it is now not very much fun travelling 2nd class, let alone 3rd!!

In the circs decided to have a ride on the Rapido which was supposed to be 1st and 2nd class. At the station I found that it was only 1st class, and as I was not prepared to throw £2 away, I decided to go on the next express.

This was a washout. Had to wait 70 mins in Bologna and an hour at Prato. Might just as well have taken a later train.

By now, the weather was back to normal. Brilliant sunshine of Italy that we know so well. The "mac" became an encumbrance. Everyone was in summer dress.

Finally arrived at Pistoia at 8.20p.m. It had taken me over 8 hours, and I was somewhat fed up. Came out of the station and recognised Paul's motor scooter, but his Brother was on it. Re-introduced myself with difficulty, and then Johanna (Paul's fiancée) turned up. She had come on the same train as me!

Without thought I said I had carried the mac long enough, and handed it to Johanna. She knew all about it. Then she informed me that Paul was in Germany (Manheim) and would not be back until Saturday.

I began to wonder if I had now lost both the mac, and the ten guineas and then I realized that of course he cannot renege his position.

I would simply notify the Company of course.

Anyway Johanna seemed to think it was a wonderful coat and I suggested that the best way to carry it was for Paul's brother to wear it. But she would have none of this. So she made off on the scooter with it over her arm.

I am not really a bit worried about the money, but it does mean that whatever happens, I must stay here until Saturday, and I suppose that means Saturday night.

Have just now had a meal and I couldn't care less about the ritual, I've had just wot I want and not bothered a bit about the menu, and local custom.

I've had <u>cold</u> roast beef, veal, and tongue, in jelly and salad, with rolls and butter and nothing more.

Now I'm just having a pot of tea. I have started a bottle of white wine, which always seems to send me a little dizzy.

Don't think I shall ever get used to it.

Hope you will have written here darling, because I expect that by the time you get this, I shall be near to starting back to Milan.

All my love darling. More tomorrow when I know the strength.

Your own

Ken xxxx

Hotel Milan, Pistoia

My Darling,

I expect you'll feel a bit fed up on Monday, but never mind, I am bringing you a little souvenir or two to make up for it. It seems fantastic really. 18 years. I can't hardly believe it. Well we cannot grumble darling, it hasn't been too bad, has it. I hope this letter is timed right dear. You should get it on Monday.

Of course, these people have fooled us. Those axles are coming along, but they are <u>not</u> drivers. So in my opinion it was necessary to wait. Nothing will be gained at all.

However it has taken until now to clear up the other fiasco, so it only means killing Sat and Sun.

Saturday is Fiesta! They will all either go mad and dance round the streets – or stay in bed – making love. (Good idea.) I don't know which yet.

Last night I went to pics to see a silent film. 30 years old! Chas Chaplin in "Modern Times" with Paulette Goddard as a girl of 14!

I still think he's just as funny. The only snag was that they stopped the film in the middle to show the 3,000,000 lire T.V. quiz, on which Italians are crazy. This caused the picture to finish at 11.50p.m.

I then went to bed, and altho' I have not been sleeping well, I never woke until 11.45a.m. today. I have made a brief visit to the works where all is finished temporarily.

This afternoon I am going shopping and I shall almost certainly get some Xmas cards. Any extra required will do at the last minute.

I am not prepared to spend money just for the sake of it, or to carry a load of junk home. And I shall be pretty well loaded by the time I have the liquor, etc. with my small bag.

I shall bring a present for you for the 10th. And something for the "house". Apart from that, I will bring cash, which is always useful.

By the way, I understand we get holiday from Fri till Thursday this year!

I don't know whether that blasted van will still be at Aston after all this time, but I think, rather hope, it has been given to someone else. At the same time of course half a loaf is better than no bread.

I have sent to that firm in Manchester for a Battery Charger, and it should arrive from Wednesday onwards.

Paul is giving me a pair of Wind Tone Horns. New. Ex U.S.A. stock. Apparently he has several sets, and has no use for them. In that case, I could afford any duty that may be charged.

The other night we went out to dinner. Paul, Johanna (his wife), an Indian inspector, and some other Italian woman (bought along because she spoke perfect English!) We had a fairly good evening which was occupied mainly with eating, drinking and talking for about 3 hours. Paul ferried us all to the restaurant on his scooter, as his car was lent out, and we all arrived at different times. But at the end there were 5 people and one scooter. So I said we would all get on like the R.A.S.G trick team – and I would drive!

The RASG trick bike team.
Ken wanted to recreate this stunt in Austria in 1955

Actuallemente they all cleared off and left me. So after much trouble in starting this cold motor I was careering around Pistoia at midnight on my own. Eventually I found the Milano, and some time later they turned up and we had a Cognac to finish up with.

Paul then took both girls home on the scooter, whilst we (Indian) fell into bed, and Finito!

That seems to be about all for now darling. Keep smiling, I hope to see you before the week is out. And I am looking forward to it a lot. Hope all the nibs are going on O.K., and that they have done O.K. in the exams. I have not seen a paper for 9 days, so I don't know how things are.

Lots of love tonight Darling

Your very own,

Ken xxxxx

Ken thought that Ivy would be a bit 'fed up' as she was having to spend yet another wedding anniversary on her own. It is endearing to read that Ken thought it was fantastic to have been married to one another for eighteen years and that they 'couldn't grumble and that it hadn't been too bad'. When all is said and done they had been through some really difficult and testing times.

The Wind Tone Horns that Ken mentions were Maserati Air Horns, which made a fabulous sound. They were used by him for many years and moved from car to car. They are still about somewhere stored amongst the family heirlooms.

Hotel Milano, Pistoia

Well Darling,

Fun and games. Altho' I had arranged last week to be here on the 22nd, they telegraphed Milan yet again the other day. I confirmed that I would get here. But on arrival that same little feller tried to cause trouble. He said the visit must be postponed because a Fork Lift truck had broken down and they could not move the axles.

I again saw the Director and Played hell. I told 'em to manhandle them, or get a mule and drag 'em round. In the finish they did this, and we got started – very rapid.

Actually it now looks as if I shall finish on Monday night and then have to kill time until Friday.

After this present visit one more trip will finish the job and it will probably take less than two weeks. And that's the end of Italy until Sept or October!

I have eaten something which has upset me, I developed an awful tummy ache and "screamers" – don't know how to spell the other word! So I went to bed at 4p.m. yesterday and stayed until 9a.m. today – and starved. Had a poached egg for breakfast and felt O.K.

Then at lunch I just had a quarter roast chicken, lettuce and a pear and banana. And now I've got it again!

Looks as if I'll have to starve again tonight!

I shouldn't write again darling after you get this because if I finish on Monday night, I shall certainly clear out of Pistoia on Tuesday morning. I will see B.E.A. in Florence about an earlier plane, but I know this is hopeless unless there is a cancellation, which I doubt.

So I may travel to Milan in 3 short hops stopping overnight on the way.

I got your letter today darling which always bucks me up. Yes H. did say come back 28th or 29th, but I couldn't get a ride. The first available date was 30th. Anyway B.T. holiday is Mon and Tues as you should know. What I hoped for was to win Friday as well.

Knew damn well the Pru would cause a muck up. However you got the cash so that's all that matters.

Wot about our old Austins?

Don't know what to think about Linda's dances. Where can they go? There don't seem to be anything left for decent folk.

So now you know wot Madge is like! P'raps you'll understand how I feel now. It just seems a waste of time to me, unless you get some fun out of it.

Post Office stuff is Bank Books. Lewis's is half-yearly statement I expect.

The Monsoon has started again and we've had torrential rain for 3 days. Terrible. Get soaked in a few yards. The yards at the factory are like a damned farmyard with white mud everywhere. No paving at all.

If you think the Easter weather will be anything like, you'd better make any plans you like to go out. Percy? Frank? Just whatever you like.

Lots of love darling

Soon be with you

Your own

Ken xxx

Ivy and Ken were concerned about the safety of their girls as they grew into young ladies. It seems that Linda wanted to go dancing; she was seventeen. There were local dances held at both Aston Commercial School and at Goodwin's in

Livingstone Road. Linda went to both venues at various times. She was a very good dancer and bought special shoes with suede on the soles to prevent slipping on the dance floor.

Madge remains a mystery; it is not known who she was or how she caused an upset. She could have been a partner at the Laura Dixon School of Dance or someone with whom Ivy and Ken played cards.

26th May 1957

Albergo Ristorante Bologna
Mestre

My Darling,

Well here I am in Mestre which is 5 miles from Venice. It is 9p.m. and I am sitting outside writing this altho' it is actually dark. I am supping a quarter litre of local wine which has cost me 60 lire.

This is a very good hotel, but Mestre is just an ordinary small town with nowt much to commend it.

However from the enquiries I have made, it is <u>out of the question</u> to stay in Venice or Venice Lido, so we'll have to put up with this.

We can either go into Venice on Train or Bus, and we'll have to carry our belongings in Beach Bags or something. Or we can go as far as the Venice car parks in the cars.

I will decide this later. Meanwhile, I have been to the Hotel recommended by Guiseppi and had an evening meal.

I really went to town and had "the lot" and it cost me 12/6d. which for Italy is reasonable. The same meal in Milano would have cost me 25/-.

I then had a look round the place and saw the rooms. They are not bad at all, and the restaurant by our standards is first class.

The boss agreed to take us for 1700 lire each per day for Dinner, Bed, Breakfast, Wine, Tax and Service included. Frankly I think this is very good, so I have booked the rooms for 28/29/30th August.

This looks like:	Room	9.0
	Wine & Dinner	7.6
	Breakfast	3.0

		19.6
		====

154

Since B & B in U.K. is 20-25/- anywhere, I don't think we can grumble.

Of course if we decided we liked it we could stop longer if <u>the rooms are free</u> but I think 2 days will be enough.

We want to get into Austria where it is cheaper, I think.

But if you see Perce and Lil, don't let 'em get any ideas that Venice is cheap. It isn't. I met an American today who is going to pay £7 per day in Hotel Europa!

So according to this we shan't do so badly.

I am going to wander round Venice tomorrow, and I'll let you know more about it then.

Meanwhile, darling, if I don't manage to get a card tomorrow, don't be too upset. I am thinking about you, and I wish you were here.

A happy Birthday darling, from

Your very own

Ken xxx

A postcard of Venice that Ken used as a
birthday card for Ivy in 1957 – she was 44

There is much in this letter about the planned second grand tour of Europe. Ken was determined to take his family to Venice as the highlight of the trip, despite the expense and the high-priced accommodation.

Ivy, Ken and three* of their girls did get to Venice and were held spellbound by it all – St Mark's Square, Doge's Palace, Clock Tower, Rialto Bridge, Bridge of Sighs and the Grand Canal.

Ken took his family by water taxi to the Murano glass factory where the owner declared himself dazzled by the little English sisters. He gave each of the girls fragile prancing glass horses and end-of-the-day baubles made of many-hued strands of coloured glass. He told Ivy and Ken that their girls were treasures beyond price. A lovely memory.

* Linda did not make the trip as she was on a foreign exchange holiday to her pen-pal in France.

Hotel Milano, Pistoia   Wednesday June 1957

My Darling,

I love you a lot tonight because when I arrived here this evening the first thing they gave me was a letter from you. And it was a very big thrill.

I have managed to borrow this machine but the keyboard is even different from the German, so I expect you'll find a lot of errors.

Sat, Mon, and Tuesday I spent in Venice and although the weather was dull or raining for the first couple of days, I found it very interesting. I think you will love it. I have spent a small fortune in finding the way about, but it will save both time and <u>our</u> money in August. I have found a good place to eat fairly reasonably well. We must make up our minds to really enjoy this. We are very, very lucky. I can see now, that in the main, it is only miserable looking old fogies that get to Venice. You know, like Daisy, and Mrs Cowper, our Mom, etc. (I didn't say your Mom!!!!)

In other words they cannot come until they have made their pile, too late to have the energy to enjoy it!!!

The prop of the restaurant put me onto a Pensione in Venice right in the centre of the place and it is going to cost us 1625 lire each for Bed and Breakfast; Tax and Service included. For Venice, this is fantastic; believe you me. In facto, Damn that is Italian, it will cost us 30 shillings each for each day in Venice. This will include all very good food, and rooms, and I repeat for Venice it is very reasonable. I have included in those figures the cost of parking the cars for two days; and the boat fares to and from the digs. Of course any other trips will be extra. But they are very cheap.

So can you tell Percy if you see him what it's going to cost him. And don't let's have any moans. They come in millions even from as far as Japan to see Venice. (And smell it!)

157

Second thoughts on the Alberoni which is at the end of the Lido Island.

I am told by an Italian that this is <u>the place</u> to go if we wish to swim/sunbathe. The Venetia Lido is for the gullible rich tourists. Ha.Ha.Ha. It makes you laugh. A Gondolier is the richest man in Italy: he only makes anything from <u>seventy to one hundred pounds per week</u>!!! It is the biggest racket I have ever come across yet!!

So we shall <u>not</u> repeat <u>not</u> be seeing Percy in a Gondole. The Gondoles are only for the suckers.

There is such a lot to tell darling, but the Hotel wants the machine back so we will have to call it a day I am afraid. I love you very much darling and am eager to see you.

But it will not be long now. I expect to be here for a few days and then back to Milan where I shall have to make a 10 minute call at Breda. And then Home. I shall probably have to wait a day or so for a 'plane, so perhaps I can <u>arrange</u> to lengthen the Whitsun Holiday and add to the fiddle which we are going to need in the Summer.

All my Love darling,

Your Very Own,
Ken xxxxx

I have spelt Gondole correctly!

Love

<u>Ken X</u>

Unusually, the final letter was typewritten on a machine borrowed from the hotel that Ken was staying in. He was still doing price-checking research in readiness for the second grand tour. It is charming that he explains to Ivy how very, very lucky they are to be going to Venice whilst they are still young.

He leaves nothing out of the calculations and expects Ivy to get her brother, Percy, up to the mark about the cost of it all and to offer no complaint.

DARLING IVY

My Darling,

I love you a lot tonight because when I arrived here this evening the first thing they gave me was a letter from you. And it was a very big thrill.

I have amanaged to borrow this machine bu the keyboard is even different from the German, so I expect you'll find a lot of errors.

Sat, Mon, and Tuesday; I spent in Venice. and althoght the weather was dull or raining for the first couple of days, I found it very interesting. I think you will all love it. I have spent a small fortune in finding the way about, but it will save both time and _our_ money in August. I have found a good place to eat fairly reasonably and well. We must make up our minds to really enjoy this. We are very, very; lucky. I can see now; that in the main it is only miserable looking old fogies that get to Venice. You know; like Daisy, and Mrs Cowper, our Mom, etc., (_I didn't say your mom.!//_)

In other words they cannot come until they have made their pile, too late to have the energy to enjoy it/: ////

The prop of the restaurant put me onto a Pensione in Venice RIGHT IN THE CENTRE of the place and it is going to cost us 1625 lire each for Bed and Breakfast; Tax and Service included. For Venice, this is fantastic; believe you me. In facto, Damn that is Italian, it will cost us 30 shillings each for each day in Venice. This will include all very good food, and rooms, and I repeat for Venice it is very reasonable. I have included in those figures the cost of parking the cars for two days; and the boat fares to and from the digs. Of course any other trips will be extra. But they are very cheap.

So you can tell Percy if you see him what it's going to cost him. And don't let's have any moans. They come in millions even from as far as Japan to see Venice. 5 (And smell it!)

Second thoughts on the Alberoni which is at the end of the Lido Island. I am told by an Italian that this is _the place_ to go if we wish to swim/sunbathe. /The Lido is for the gullible (_Venetians_) rich tourists. Ha. Ha. Ha; It makes you laugh. A Gondolier is the richest man in Italy.:::::://////::::: He only makes anything from seventy to one hundred,pounds per week. ////

It is the biggest racket I have ever come across yet//////

So we shall not repeat not be seeing Percy in a Gondole.

Gondoles are only for the suckers.

There is such a lot to tell darling, but the Hotel wants the machine back so we will have to call it a day I am afraid.

I love you very much darling and am eager to see you.

But it will not be long now. I expect to be here for a few days and then back to Milan where I shall have to make a 10 minute call at Breda. Q And then HoMe////. I shall probably have to wait a day or so for a 'plane, so perhaps I can arrange to lengthen the Whitsun Holiday and add to the fiddle which we are going to need in the Summer.

All my Love darling,

Your Very Own,

Ken XXX

I have spelt Gondole correctly!

Love Ken x

The letter is peppered with exclamation marks and under-lining, as well as numerous annotations in blue biro. Ken made sure that Ivy knew that he had not misspelled 'Gondole'. Was he trying to impress her with his use of the Italian spelling?

Ken's daughters love this letter – it shows his excitement, his organisational skills, his enthusiasm, his love for his family, his humour, his ingenuity and his eccentricity in great abundance.

Austria, 1957 – Second European Grand Tour
Standing, left to right: Ivy, Muriel, Ken, Lil
Front row, left to right: Lorna, Jen, Pam

Postscript

Ken died on 3 May 1977 in the way that he wanted, doing what he loved the best.

'I hope I snuff it before I'm too old or too ill to know what I'm doing' was his oft-heard refrain.

In the event he simply came in from the garden, sat in his favourite chair and 'snuffed' it – just like that.

It was a profound shock for Ivy and the girls, but knowing that he had had his wish consoled them. He had vanished much too soon and his presence is still felt each and every day, in some small way, by his daughters.

Ivy, of course, never completely recovered from his loss and remained alone for the rest of her life.

Ivy died 29 years later in 2005, surrounded by her four daughters and with a favourite photograph of Ken close by. The girls, as usual, were chatting to Ivy even though she could no longer respond with words. They were talking animatedly about Ivy's granddaughter's forthcoming wedding. As they talked Ivy slipped peacefully away, dreaming of wedding hats, and shoes, and flowers and honeymoons.

How fitting that another love story was just beginning as Ivy and Ken's drew gently to a close.